COMMON QUESTIONS ON SCHIZOPHRENIA AND THEIR ANSWERS

KEATS TITLES OF RELATED INTEREST

Brain Allergies by William H. Philpott, M.D. and
Dwight K. Kalita, Ph.D.

Diet and Disease by E. Cheraskin, M.D., D.M.D.,
W. M. Ringsdorf, D.M.D. and J. W. Clark, D.D.S.

The Healing Nutrients Within by Eric R. Braverman, M.D. with
Carl C. Pfeiffer, Ph.D., M.D.

Mental and Elemental Nutrients by Carl C. Pfeiffer, Ph.D., M.D.

Nutrients to Age Without Senility by Abram Hoffer, M.D., Ph.D.
and Morton Walker, D.P.M.

The Nutrition Desk Reference by Robert H. Garrison, Jr., R.Ph.,
and Elizabeth Somer, M.A.

Orthomolecular Nutrition by Abram Hoffer, M.D., Ph.D. and
Morton Walker, D.P.M.

Physician's Handbook on Orthomolecular Medicine edited by
Roger Williams, Ph.D. and Dwight K. Kalita, Ph.D.

COMMON QUESTIONS ON SCHIZOPHRENIA AND THEIR ANSWERS

Abram Hoffer, M.D., Ph.D.

Keats Publishing, Inc. ▓ New Canaan, Connecticut

Library of Congress Cataloging-in-Publication Data

Hoffer, Abram, 1917–
   Common questions on schizophrenia and their answers.

   Bibliography: p.
   Includes index.
   1. Schizophrenia—Popular works.   2. Schizophrenia—
Treatment.   3. Orthomolecular therapy.   I. Title.
[DNLM: 1. Schizophrenia—therapy—popular works.
WM 203 H698c]
RC514.H565   1987   616.89'82   87-21392
ISBN 0-87983-378-5 (pbk.)

Printed in the United States of America

Keats Publishing, Inc.
27 Pine Street
New Canaan, Connecticut 06840

CONTENTS

To my wife Rose
an unfailing support
a timely solace
a constant joy

and

to
John, Myrna, TL
and all the other
schizophrenia patients
I have been privileged
to help and to learn from

COMMON QUESTIONS ON SCHIZOPHRENIA AND THEIR ANSWERS

Preface

Schizophrenia has been and is one of the most fearful of diseases. Even the words used to diagnose it strike terror into the minds of patients and their families. And why not? How can anyone not be afraid of the term *dementia praecox*—premature or early-onset dementia? It would frighten the hell out of me. Replacing it with *schizophrenia* was an improvement, but not much. Would anyone want to have a split mind?—the common, if erroneous, interpretation.

The stigma of schizophrenia is powerful and pervasive. Patients were fearful of being told, even when they suspected it. Psychiatrists were fearful of telling them, preferring to hide behind less stigmatized words. Institutions which housed patients soon were stigmatized as much as their patients, and the stigma permeated the entire psychiatric profession until it spread from mental hospitals to private practice, and to other types of patients. Hospital administrators knew patients abhorred their hospitals and dealt with this by changing the name: asylums became mental hospitals, which in turn became state or psychiatric hospitals. It made little difference, since patients were fearful not of the name but what it signified. There was little change in the institutions or type of treatment. At University Hospital, Saskatoon, Saskatchewan, the psychiatric patients were treated on the fifth floor, wards D and E—5 DE. The stigma was on 5 DE almost from the day this hospital opened; patients did not want to go to the psychiatric ward or 5 DE.

There has been some improvement over the past two decades, and patients and families are less fearful than they were, but more must be done. It is important to understand why the stigma was sensed and how it can be removed.

There are two main reasons why there was so much fear. First, schizophrenia was excluded from the Medical Model (a term I shall explore in detail later). It was not a disease like diabetes, or tuberculosis, or diptheria, or like other "medical" diseases. It was a disease of the mind, or of the person, or a failure of will or of personality. Schizophrenics were weak-willed, or born inferior, or did not try hard enough. They were mental, psychological or social misfits, or failures (as in fact many were, *because* they were sick). They were seen as seeking the truth by becoming schizophrenic, or as trying to protect sick families by taking the burden on themselves. They were forced into schizophrenia by mothers or by fathers, or even by grandmothers, or by communities. Hundreds of explanations were invoked, especially at the height of psychoanalysis. The disease, however, remained mysterious, both to patients and their doctors, and was denied the privilege of being a medical disease within the Medical Model.

Ironically, psychiatrists were doomed to remain the custodians of the insane outside the Medical Model, for as soon as a cause was discovered and treatment developed, schizophrenia was promptly reclassified and taken over by "real" doctors—neurologists and general practitioners. Schizophrenics who were ill because they had spirochetes in their brain were seen as suffering from general paresis of the insane and were treated by antibiotics. Schizophrenics who were pellagrins disappeared when vitamin B3 came into use fifty years ago; there is no stigma attached to pellagra. Recently, the very intelligent father of a schizophrenic girl told his friends she has pellagra. He could not tolerate the idea that she was schizophrenic.

The second reason was the absence of effective treatment. The early medical treatments such as insulin coma, ECT ("shock treatments"), and later tranquilizers, were helpful but only to a small proportion of patients. These treatments did at times reduce the intensity of symptoms but were more helpful to mental hospital administrators than to the patients, families or the community.

Society will stigmatize any condition which is outside of the Medical Model and for which there is no effective treatment. AIDS is a recent example of a very serious disease which so far has escaped the stigma attached to schizophrenia. It is firmly entrenched in the Medical Model with a known cause, even without any effective treatment. Yet AIDS is a lifestyle disease whch can be avoided in most cases. The epidemic of AIDS has generated a good deal of sympathy and has mobilized the public and medical science to search for a treatment.

Dr. Humphry Osmond and I began our battle to remove the stigma from schizophrenia in 1960 when we proposed that all patients be told they had schizophrenia. Later in our book, *How to Live with Schizophrenia*, we outlined the first comprehensive biochemical theory of schizophrenia. We suggested that it was a disease caused by excessive oxidation of adrenalin to adrenochrome. In modern terms, this is a free-radical theory. We also reported that vitamin B3 and vitamin C were more effective than other treatments when used in optimal doses. Later, Osmond and M. Siegler analyzed the theory of the Medical Model. In a series of papers, lectures and a fine book, *Models of Madness, Models of Medicine*, they showed how only the Medical Model adequately met the needs of patient, family and community.

We also organized the Canadian Schizophrenia Foundation and the American Schizophrenia Association. The latter became the Huxley Institute for Biosocial Research. These two organizations have disseminated information in North America to their members and the public by means of reports, reprints, books and meetings, and the *Journal of Orthomolecular Psychiatry*, (now the *Journal of Orthomolecular Medicine*). In my opinion, these organizations have played a major role in bringing schizophrenia back into medicine and in demystifying the disease. Our main objective has been to provide accurate information about schizophrenia, especially about treatment. We have demanded that treatment must be better. Unlike other mental health organizations which tried to persuade families and the community to tolerate bad behavior, we have tried to educate them to demand more effective treatment. Instead of demanding more hospitals, more medical and nursing staff, and more money, we have demanded they use the best treatments available.

Today, schizophrenia appears firmly entrenched in the Medical Model, but most psychiatrists pay only lip service to the concept. They are still reluctant to discuss the diagnosis, to describe the current theories of cause, and to use specific treatment. Tranquilizers are okay because all know they are merely superior sedatives, and thus can be used as aids to psychotherapy. Vitamins are not drugs. Any psychiatrist using nutrients is forced to accept that they are involved in the causes. No one believes schizophrenia is caused by an inborn deficiency of any tranquilizer.

There is no reason for any stigma. Schizophrenia is a disease like any other, and has a treatment which is as successful as treatment is for many diseases, and more successful than the treatment of some, such as arthritis.

This book is another step toward removing the stigma from schizophrenia. It is a disease like any other, with the target organ the brain rather than the lungs or heart. But by attacking the biochemistry of the brain it changes personality and behavior, and so distorts the victims that they may become strangers even to their parents.

The stigma, unreasonable shame and fear of schizophrenia will be overcome. Then we can proceed to the final solution—prevention.

People who read this book will be armed with information with which they can free themselves from guilt and prejudice. Patients will demand more effective treatment in settings where they are not stripped of their dignity. They will know their rights, but even more important, their responsibilities, for recovering from schizophrenia requires the cooperation of patient, family, community and doctor, all working and knowing they are working within the Medical Model.

Schizophrenia is a disease of the body affecting the brain, which is the leading organ of the body. It is not a disease of the mind.

In order to highlight the information in this book I have written it as if I were having a very long conversation with an intelligent patient who has recovered from schizophrenia. This patient has outlined all the important questions about which s/he was puzzled and has then written this book. I have, in fact, had a conversation with myself. I have learned about schizophrenia from my own experiences with hallucinogenic drugs such as LSD and from my thousands of patients until, I believe, I can think and reason like a schizophrenic.

What Is Schizophrenia?

Dr. Hoffer, what is schizophrenia? From what I've read and heard people say, I get the idea that it's something like a split personality.

Schizophrenia is a disease affecting the whole body, but most evident in its effects on the patient's attitudes and perceptions. What is observed or heard is misunderstood or misperceived, thought processes are disordered, and there may be hallucinations or delusions.

The word has led to a lot of confusion about the disease. Many do indeed think it means a split personality, with one of a number of apparently different personalities emerging from one person, much as in *The Three Faces of Eve*. This is not schizophrenia and is quite rare, whereas schizophrenia attacks up to three percent of populations. Others use schizophrenia inappropriately as a pejorative adjective to describe someone who has two opposing views of the same topic. They refer to politicians, writers, and so on, as showing schizophrenic switches in ideas. Schizophrenics do not hold two opposing views simultaneously. On the contrary, schizophrenic ideas, especially delusions, are held with great tenacity and consistency as long as the illness persists. To label a politician schizophrenic is as inappropriate as it would be to describe his ideas and attitude as diabetic or nephritic.

So why is the term schizophrenia used?

The word-root *schizo* means "to split" or "a splitting." But Bleuler, its inventor, referred to dissociation between mood and thought, not to a splitting of the mind. People who have been ill a long time may develop a mood, emotion or feeling which is inappropriate to their thinking or to their social setting. This is rare, but when it does occur is most often expressed as inappropriate laughing or giggling in a setting where this would be most unusual or surprising. Depression is seldom one of the inappropriate moods.

How many people have schizophrenia?

At least one percent of the population. As diagnosis is difficult and the disease is often not recognized, I believe it would be safe to put it at three percent.

Is it one of those diseases you find more of in industrialized, prosperous countries, like heart disease and some kinds of cancer?

The incidence seems to be the same throughout the industrialized world and to manifest itself similarly everywhere. Until recently, psychiatrists believed that the same proportion of any population became ill throughout history. However, reviews of much better recent epidemiological data show that it was quite rare before 1800 and has since increased rapidly, but only in industrialized nations. It is still rare among native populations which retain their old ways, as it probably was among ancient Athenians or Romans or Elizabethan English. Like many of the diseases which plague us today, it is a disease endemic to industrialized countries.

If it's that common, I'm surprised that the psychiatrist I saw some years ago wouldn't even mention schizophrenia to me. Why was that? Do medical schools teach them to avoid talking about it to their patients?

Schizophrenics are not kept in ignorance as much now as they were twenty-five years ago. Until 1960 it was standard procedure *not* to tell patients they had schizophrenia. This "do-not-tell" movement reached its zenith with Dr. Karl Menninger's paper in which he advised psychiatrists never to tell their patients because knowing would be so harmful to the patient. Of course he meant well. The word may well have frightened patients. It certainly did frighten the psychiatrists, who became very adept not only in denying the diagnosis to their patients, but also to themselves. Schizophrenics do not respond to psychotherapy devoid of biochemical treatment components. Psychiatrists who hoped psychotherapy would help deferred making the diagnosis until the expression of the illness made continued self-delusion impossible. The do-not-tell movement reflected not only a desire to avoid harming patients but also the need to avoid frightening the psychiatrists. I recall an incident in 1953: A young resident in psychiatry had been giving his young female patient psychotherapy in hospital for many weeks, having diagnosed her an anxiety state; then I interviewed her to see if she was appropriate for one of our research studies. During the interview she would frequently look over her shoulder to a corner of the room. Finally I asked her what she was looking at. She replied that her sister, who normally lived in Edmonton, was now perched on the wall looking down at her! The resident had neglected to ask her about hallucinations. At that time psychiatrists were convinced that patients should not be asked direct questions about hallucinations. It was feared the patient would promptly make up or imagine them—that suggestion was so powerful it would induce the phenomenon. If patients described their hallucinations without any questioning or prodding, then they were really there. I reported her visions to her resident, who was forced to rediagnose her. He immediately stopped giving her psychotherapy, and a few days later she was transferred to a mental hospital.

Do you mean to tell me psychiatrists are afraid to tell their patients that they have schizophrenia?

This fear of schizophrenia was demonstrated very convincingly in 1967 at a conference at Napa State Hospital in California. I had been asked to address a meeting of residents, psychiatrists, other staff and community physicians, as well as family members who were interested in improving treatment for schizophrenia. Other speakers were the director of training for that hospital, and two professors of psychiatry.

After our presentations we acted as a panel to interact with the meeting.

Sitting in the front row was a physician who was very unhappy with the results of treating his schizophrenic wife. He had spoken to me about it before the meeting. He was up first to ask a question. Very loudly he said, "Dr. Hoffer, this question is not for you. You are not to answer it. It is for the other three on the platform." Then he directed his question to the professor on my immediate left. "Professor ——," he said, "would you ever tell a patient of yours she or he had schizophrenia?" The professor blanched and refused to answer. The irate physician shouted at him to answer the question, but the professor sat silent. At last the physician turned to the next one, who laughed and replied that he would not tell the patient, but would tell him or her they "were nuts." The third member replied that he would not use the word schizophrenia either, but would use something like "emotionally disturbed." In my presentation I had made a strong statement that every patient had a right to know what the diagnosis was.

Have you done anything about that?

About 1960, Dr. Humphry Osmond and I began to recommend that all patients be given their diagnosis. A few years later we released our book *How to Live with Schizophrenia**, which made it possible for the first time for patients and their families to learn what disease they were suffering. Today it is unusual for patients not to be told, but they are still not given all the information they ought to have. In October 1984, a mother from Alberta wrote to me about her son after she read our book. She wrote, "as you described, our experience has been with psychiatrists who refused to diagnose our son's illness. They won't label him." He first became ill in 1978. In 1980, a University of Alberta psychiatrist finally told them his diagnosis.

---

*Hoffer, A. and Osmond, H., *How to Live With Schizophrenia*. University Books, Inc., New York, 1966, 1978.

I suspected I was schizophrenic and was very frightened, especially when my psychiatrist would not talk about it.

The diagnosis is important because it allows you to come to grips with the nature of the disease, the treatment and the prognosis. Merely telling the patient he has schizophrenia is not enough, for it may mobilize all the incomplete or erroneous information he has acquired in the past. This is why it is so harmful for patients to learn about their diagnosis by other means. In my opinion, most schizophrenics even in 1960 knew the name of their disease and they were just as fearful of it as their psychiatrists were. One of my patients had shot himself after reading his file. He had had three admissions to a university hospital. After his last admission he was discharged on tranquilizers and referred back to his general practitioner. Several weeks later when he was in his doctor's office the doctor was called out, leaving his file on his desk. The patient promptly looked at it and for the first time knew he had been diagosed schizophrenic. At home that day he looked it up in a dictionary and read that it was a chronic, incurable disease. The next day he shot himself with a rifle, missing his heart by half an inch.

I tried to sneak a look at my chart when I was in hospital to see what I had been diagnosed as having. Is that unusual?

Patients use many strategies for finding out their diagnosis if their psychiatrists will not tell them. Here are a few of them:

Reading one's own chart. This is a regular occurrence in mental hospitals. Every intelligent patient will do so.

Getting information from one's spouse after the psychiatrist has informed the spouse, cautioning secrecy. In one case the husband was given the diagnosis; on the way home he passed on to his wife what he had been told.

Finding out from insurance forms.

One Boston patient was refused his diagnosis by six different psychoanalysts. He had letterhead paper printed as if he were a physician, wrote to each analyst requesting his diagnosis and received six replies, each reporting that he was schizophrenic.

Do you also talk with your patients about the disease and its prognosis?

As soon as the diagnosis is given, I inform the patient that the condition is not mental but is a physical, or biochemical, or metabolic disease which causes psychiatric symptoms. I will then offer a brief or detailed outline of the perceptual theory of schizophrenia as outlined in *How to Live with Schizophrenia*. Very few psychiatrists give their patients any explanation about schizophrenia except perhaps to call it a chemical imbalance.

Finally, after discussing treatment, I offer them a prognosis, indicating how long it will take for them to recover if they are able to follow the treatment process.

Patients who know what is wrong and know something about their illness have a much better chance of getting well. They will also seek treatment earlier and demand they be referred to a psychiatrist earlier, for the sooner treatment is started, the better the chances that it will be effective.

Is there such a thing as a personality type that's predisposed to schizophrenia? Could I have been spotted as being likely to become a schizophrenic?

No. Schizophrenics are represented in all personality types, although there is much belief in the "schizoid personality," ingoing, introverted, quiet and preferring seclusion.

Children of this type were considered to be at risk for schizophrenia, and their parents were warned to be on the alert for this. However, studies undertaken to test the concept showed that introverts developed schizophrenia no more frequently that other personality types. I suspect that this confusion arose from mistaking early signs of the disease for the preexisting personality type—something like saying that a "sneezing personality" is likely to develop a cold. Since the disease comes on insidiously and slowly, without sudden obvious symptoms such as weight loss or fever, it is easy to see how this could happen. But there is no such thing as a "schizoid personality," and the term might as well be dropped.

If personality type isn't a clue, what are the warning signs, the first hints that someone might be developing schizophrenia?

Not personality type, but personality change, is the hallmark of schizophrenia. If a person's character changes markedly, and there is no apparent cause, such as an illness or a significant change in his or her personal environment, schizophrenia should be considered as a possibility.

Since you have to have a sense of what the personality changed from, people with some years of developed personal history are easier to diagnose than those with very little or who are still developing. For this reason schizophrenia is difficult to diagnose in children and adolescents, especially since schizophrenic personality changes can be mistaken for normal adolescent behavior. It is also easy to miss development of schizophrenia in women immediately after they have given birth, when the illness can be mistaken for "normal" depression, and in the extremely aged, in whom a variety of possible "senile" conditions makes accurate diagnosis difficult.

It couldn't be called good news, but my family was at least relieved to know about my diagnosis after so many years of uncertainty.

Families with a history of mental illness or breakdown are more vulnerable to additional breakdown. They should learn as much as possible about schizophrenia by reading the few books which describe it for lay people. Then they should compare their own symptoms with the descriptions in these books. Finally, they could quantify their own symptoms by using the HOD test. *

The symptoms may be classified into general symptoms which indicate one is not well but which may be associated with other diseases, and into specific symptoms which suggest schizophrenia is present.

What are some of the main general symptoms of schizophrenia?

First is fatigue. This comes on slowly, is present for a long time although it may fluctuate, and cannot be explained by overwork, unusual stress or other diseases. The relationship to stress may not be clear since any person is less able to cope with stress when ill and may blame the stress when not aware the problem is in the person. Burnout has become a popular word for chronic fatigue. Usually the reason given is overwork in a demanding job such as air traffic controller, nurse, doctor, etc. The fatigue associated with schizophrenia is like a burnout without any external or psychosocial reason.

Then there are mood disorders such as depression, rapid mood swings and anxiety. The mood swings are different from manic-depressive mood swings. Sadly, the patient may spend much time in psychotherapy, "talking through" his problems with the therapist and becoming increasingly frightened as no progress is made. Psychoanalytic methods are just not effective with schizophrenia, and reliance on them is a serious barrier to dealing with the disease effectively.

I tried that for a while, and, you're right, it didn't get me anywhere with the depression. But then I got really scared when I began seeing flashing lights that weren't there, and people's faces, even the ones I knew well, looked like someone else. Is that what you call a perceptual disorder?

*Hoffer, A., Kelm, H. and Osmond, H., *The Hoffer-Osmond Diagnostic Test*. Robert E. Krieger Publishing Co., Huntington, NY 11743, 1975. HOD kit available from Rehabilitation Research Foundation, PO Box BV, University, Alabama 35486.

It is indeed, and a typical one. There are two kinds of perceptual disorders, illusions and hallucinations. Illusions are early and less vivid changes in sense perception and may affect one or more of the senses. Hallucinations are more vivid and usually more disabling perceptual changes, though illusions may be just as disabling as hallucinations, depending upon a person's occupation.

Would you describe a few illusions?

Anyone who has experienced the effect of the hallucinogens, especially LSD, will know something about illusions. They are much more common than hallucinations but are more often missed because patients may not know how to describe them or may simply say they feel unreal or that the world is unreal.

There may be changes in color, in form, in depth perception, and the visual field may become unstable. Recently a patient described how the road she was driving on began to curve upward to the sky and she could no longer judge where oncoming traffic was. She asked her husband to grab the wheel and was able to bring the car to a stop in the ditch. She gave up driving. Another patient could not carry on as a typist because she could not keep her eye on the line of words she was transcribing from. Children often find that words on a page begin to move back and forth and may even collide with each other. It then becomes very difficult to read. An early sign of visual disorder is often mistaken for needing glasses. I have seen a number of patients who had changed their glasses up to three times in one year before they were seen by a psychiatrist.

It is not possible to list all the possible illusions of our senses, but they all have one thing in common: they destabilize the experimental world. Here are some of the most frequently encountered types:

AUDITORY

Illusions shade into auditory hallucinations. Dreams in which the dreamer hears speech, music and/or other sounds are normal; the first step toward abnormality is taken when these dream illusions and hallucinations remain for awhile after the person is fully awake. This is often the first indication in children that they are seriously ill. The next phase occurs when people *hear* their own thoughts, but accept them as their thoughts. Another step toward abnormality occurs when these thoughts come from outside the person. They are now hallucinations, but often the presence of these auditory hallucinations depends upon the presence of background sounds. This may be a conversation other people are having which is heard in such a way that there is no relationship to what is actually said. One of my patients only heard voices when birds were chirping. Another heard them only when water was running from a tap. A few experiments several years ago showed that schizophrenics no longer heard voices when they were placed in a special sound-free room.

Recovery retraces these steps. When patients tell me they no longer hear voices when awake but do hear them in their dreams, I expect they are on the way to recovery.

TASTE

Taste illusions are present when foods no longer taste the way they do normally. This is the basis for the paranoid delusions that someone has tampered with the food and put poison into it. Foods taste flat, or bitter, or in many other ways different. People who are not schizophrenic may also develop taste illusions, especially if they are deficient in zinc, but they do not have a thought disorder and do not become delusional. But they may lose their appetite so severely they will stop eating. This is not uncommon in elderly people whose diets are deficient in zinc.

SMELL

Smell (olfactory) illusions are rare but often accompany taste illusions. Odors change their character. A few patients complain their own bodies have a foul smell. This may be based on reality, as many patients with schizophrenia do have an aromatic, unpleasant odor as long as they are sick. One of my female patients complained to me that the nurses were insisting she have two baths per day. She was a very clean person but did have a powerful schizophrenic odor which enveloped her, creating a smelly bubble for at least ten feet around her. I had to write an order that she was not to be forced to bathe. As she recovered, the odor vanished.

TOUCH

Tactile illusions are rare. As with the other senses, they are distortions of normal sensations.

I had some of these illusions but they were not nearly as obvious and frightening as hallucinations. Can you describe a few of these?

Hallucinations are more extreme perceptual changes and are not nearly as frequent as illusions. They are present in well-developed and chronic schizophrenia; rarely do they come early in the illness. They cover the same range as illusions.

VISUAL

Things, scenes and movement are seen which no one else can see and which the same person when well has not seen nor will see after recovery. There is a limitless range of visual hallucinations, depending only on the ability of any brain to formulate visions and on the personal experiences of that person. Patients see animals, people they have known or have never seen, angels, devils, gods, energy, scenes. One of my patients saw himself being raped by his mother's live-in boyfriend. A month after his medication was altered these hallucinations had disappeared to be replaced by vivid visualizations of women, which were, however, under his voluntary control, *i.e.*, when he thought about something else they vanished. The previous visual hallucinations came whether he was thinking or not and could not be removed; they were autonomous.

Hallucinations are *not* imaginary and cannot be suggested to the patient. For many years psychiatrists were afraid to ask patients if they hallucinated, because they believed the mere act of asking would create the phenomenon. In my experience, hallucinations are so bizarre that it is impossible to suggest them to anyone. The person simply can not understand what is to be hallucinated. Even patients who hear voices and consider this normal cannot understand other patients who see visions. Psychiatrists who have not been schizophrenic or have not experienced the effect of hallucinogenic drugs have the same difficulty understanding their patients' hallucinations. Perhaps this is why they think patients can imagine these phenomena. The vividness of hallucinations may vary from a dreamlike vision to one which is as real as anything seen in the real world.

AUDITORY

Voices are the most common auditory hallucinations, but there is no shortage of others. The range of variation is narrower than it is for visual hallucinations. They may be present continually as long as the person is awake, but usually not when asleep. Most of them occur now and then, usually at random. They may be so loud, so insistent and clear that the patient will speak back to them in a loud voice. Patients who speak to themselves may be having a conversation with their voices.

OTHER HALLUCINATIONS

Touch, smell and taste hallucinations occur in the absence of direct stimuli; *i.e.*, no one else is aware of this phenomena. Some of my patients felt fingers were touching them. Some felt worms crawling under their skin. Many were aware of strange odors no one else could smell and others had a bizarre or foul taste in their mouths even when they were not eating anything.

I was very disturbed by some of my hallucinations. How can they influence behavior so powerfully?

The impact of perceptual changes depends upon the patient's judgment as to whether these symptoms are real or not. The impact may be minimal if a judgment is made that these perceptual changes are not real—if the patient has decided that the symptoms have arisen from his own sensory system. If the person concludes that the phenomena are real, there will be major behavioral changes. How, then, does a person decide what to believe?

The ability to judge that illusions and hallucinations are not real but are the product of one's sensory system depends upon a number of factors. Experience with similar changes is very important. Once a person has experienced a variety of sensory changes and has then become normal, it is easier to judge subsequent changes as not being real. Recovered schizophrenics will find it easier to judge the new set of sensory changes as not true if they relapse. Normal subjects who have experienced the hallucinogens also find it easier to accept the phenomena as not true. I have seen a large number of early schizophrenics who had taken hallucinogens, most often LSD, many years before develop illusions which were similar to their LSD changes. They might consider these flashbacks, which they are not. I have known patients who had used the hallucinogens so frequently over many years that they became quite comfortable with the psychotic world and could function reasonably well. Psychiatrists and nurses having undergone hallucinogenic experiences who work with schizophrenics in my opinion are better able to understand their patients' perceptual symptoms. Patients appreciate having someone they can talk to freely about their perceptual symptoms. Previous experience is very important. Most psychiatrists have not experienced either schizophrenia or the hallucinogens. They can sensitize themselves to the phenomena by spending time with their patients and by reading autobiographies of schizophrenics.

Next to experience is the ability to test the truth of our observations. We all do it, adults more often than children. If we see something very unusual we will often point it out to our friends or associates and ask, "Do you see it?" If they agree, the truth of the phenomenon is confirmed. If they do not, doubt is thrown on the existence of the event. Patients deliberately test themselves, but this is usually done privately, for most people know that the experiential world should be stable and that instabilities are unusual. That is why you do not discuss voices and visions with your friends.

Children have seen shadow illusions, *i.e.*, shadows when little light is present have taken on the appearance of animals. One little boy told me about the large black bears he saw springing at him through the door at night. The children may tell their parents. Their parents are so unfamiliar with this that they will respond inappropriately by denying the phenomena, by calling it a dream, or imaginary. The child quickly realizes the illusion is something bad and causes anxiety and fear, and so will no longer talk about it. The correct response is to discuss with the child what was seen, to explain it as an illusion, a trick of the mind, something which is not evil or bad, and then to do something about it such as using a night light, reassurance and perhaps proper treatment. An adult may find foods taste bitter. He may wonder whether the food has been "doctored" or tampered with, but will soon realize no harm has come to him. Poison kills or makes one sick, and this did not happen. Therefore there was no poison; It was a taste illusion.

People test the truth of their misperceptions by running these private thought experiments. They realize that the logical consequences of these perceptual events do not follow and therefore they are not real, not true. A chronic patient described how he came to mistrust his voices and conclude they were not real. His voices continually prophesied what would happen. After a while he realized they were wrong. He therefore made a point of remembering the prophecies and noting whether any were fulfilled. They were not, so he concluded that they were not real.

Patients will ask people they trust. If this happens, it is very important that person be honest and deny the reality of the misperception. Another patient heard voices telling him to place his hand in the fire in the fireplace. Eventually he did so, burning himself severely. He had asked his brother whether the voices were real and his brother did not deny it. Later in his autobiography he described how helpful to him it would have been if his brother had been honest and had denied the reality of his voices.

I often advise my patients in the presence of their relatives to ask them if they become uncertain about their hallucinations. Their relatives act as a link between the patient and the real world.

The intensity of the perceptual symptoms also determines how their reality is judged. If they are vague and indistinct it will be much easier to judge them not true. If they are vivid and intense and are present for an appreciable period of time, they will be more difficult to judge not true.

Another factor is whether more than one sense is involved in the perceptual change. If a person sees a vision and also hears it speak, it will be more likely to be judged real than if only one sense is involved in the phenomenon. If three senses are involved, which is rare, it is almost impossible not to believe that the phenomenon is real. If the patient sees an angel, hears her speak to him and feels her fingers on his brow, he will undoubtedly believe in her reality. This has happened to several of my patients.

So the illusions and hallucinations are what goes wrong with how we experience things. What about what you call thought disorders?

There are two major types of disturbance in thinking. Most common is a change in thought content, less common is a disorder in thought process.

THOUGHT CONTENT

The most common disorders are called delusions and paranoid ideas. They may arise from the perceptual changes which are present, especially if they are judged to be real. If there is something wrong with the sensation of taste so that foods taste bitter, it is not difficult to believe someone has placed poison there, especially if the person is ill and also has a disorder of thinking or judgment. This paranoid delusion can be elaborated to the idea that a group of people are involved in a plot against the individual and that part of the plot was the poisoning of the food, which was why it tasted bitter. Delusions may be simple or complex fueled by the perceptual changes and by the decision these changes are real. A few examples will illustrate the relationship between perceptual changes and thought disorder.

1. A young schizophrenic adolescent developed the idea that everyone was looking at her all the time. In response she became fearful and seclusive, refusing to leave her room. She told me she could see lines around her eyes which made her ugly, and that was why people were looking. She was, in fact, very pretty.

2. A middle-aged woman was diagnosed as having oculogyric crises. She would now and then roll her eyes upward and backward. When I was interviewing her she did this once more. I asked her what she saw. She replied she was watching a large number of insects marching up the wall in front of her. She was merely watching a visual hallucination. She was schizophrenic, not suffering from a neurological symptom.

3. A young man told me that there was a conspiracy against him which was why he was followed no matter where he went. The same person was in a car behind him when he was being driven to my office and also sat in the waiting room beside him. It soon became clear that faces had become very indistinct and all appeared to him to be the same. This led to his conclusion that different people were the same person and logically created the belief he was the victim of a massive plot.

4. A middle-aged woman gave up driving her car after one evening when she saw the road run up into the sky in front of her.

5. A young man was visited by a large pig-like devil who ordered him to kill. A short time later he shot all but one member of a family he had never seen before.

6. A young prison inmate escaped. He had become convinced there was a plot against him to kill him. He had to escape to save his life. His evidence of the plot was poisonous smells coming from his ventilator (an olfactory change), poison in his food (taste changes) followed by nausea and vomiting when he ate the food, and whispering from guards discussing the plot (auditory hallucinations).

How can you possibly remember all the questions needed to elicit most of the perceptual symptoms and thought disorder?

Patients are generally not aware of all the perceptual symptoms they have. Often when they are aware there is something wrong they do not know how to describe them because they are so novel. For this reason, Dr. H. Osmond and I developed the simple card sorting test I mentioned earlier, the HOD (Hoffer-Osmond Diagnostic) test.

The test consists of 145 cards, each containing a question or statement. Questions concern the five perceptual senses, the presence of thinking disorder and questions about mood. Each card is placed in a "True" or "False" box by the subject. The cards placed in the true box are recorded by their number on a special scoring sheet. Scores are derived from the "True" cards. A perceptual score of more than 4 suggests that perceptual disturbances are present. The higher the score, the more of these cards declared true, the greater is the degree of perceptual disturbance and the greater the possibility schizophrenia or other perceptual diseases are present. There are also paranoid scores, depression scores and a total or global score.

The HOD test can be administered by anyone, or it can be self-administered. It has been found useful by orthomolecular physicians who want to know if perceptual changes are present. The HOD test can be helpful in the following ways:

1. As a diagnostic test. Because of the large number of question cards dealing with perception, it is a perceptual test and any condition which causes perceptual changes will be revealed by high scores. The main diseases which affect perception are schizophrenia, psychotomimetic reactions and deliria. A delirium characteristically clears fairly rapidly once the patient has been separated from the toxin and hallucinogenic (psychotomimetic) substances. Thus HOD scores which decrease quickly suggest schizophrenia is not present. The test is very useful in differentiating between mood disorders and schizophrenia. Physicians are surprised at the number of patients they had considered anxiety states or depressions who are really schizophrenic. The high scores alert them to repeat the mental status examination.

2. As an aid in psychotherapy. The type and intensity of psychotherapy must be planned with a knowledge of the perceptual disturbances. A patient preoccupied with disturbing perceptual symptoms is hardly fit to participate in intensive psychotherapy. A few enterprising psychologists are already using the test very effectively.

3. To measure the effect of treatment. As a patient improves, the scores go down. If the test is repeated every week or month, one can measure the amount of improvement and how fast it is occuring. If there is no change in scores, obviously the patient is not improving. This will be an indication for the physician to change the program to accelerate recovery. Patients do not mind doing this test repeatedly, especially when they know why it is being done. Many of my patients have asked me to repeat the test. They were eager to measure changes in themselves. Many have obtained their own test and have monitored their condition.

The HOD scores are affected by age and by the phase of the menstrual cycle. The test is not valid for children under thirteen unless they are very intelligent. When we tested large numbers of school children from grades 8 to 12, we found a striking relationship between age and scores. As children matured the HOD scores decreased. Children who were not well had higher scores and these scores decreased more slowly. Students who were older than their peers in any grade generally had higher scores while students who were younger than their peers for any grade had much lower scores. Children with scores much higher than the mean for their age were more apt to require psychiatric treatment later on.

High scores quickly decreased to normal levels if they were treated with Vitamin B3.

HOD scores fluctuate with the menstrual cycle. They are lowest at ovulation and then gradually increase, reaching their highest level during the premenstrual phase and decreasing after the period is over. More women are admitted to hospital for schizophrenia during the premenstrual phase than at other phases of the cycle.

Being a schizophrenic seems to mean living under a pretty dark cloud, and without the proverbial silver lining.

Curiously enough, schizophrenia does seem to carry with it a few genetic advantages—which is probably why it remains constant in the population, rather than decreasing. Many schizophrenics are outstandingly attractive physically, and tend to age and go gray more slowly than others. They are also remarkably tolerant of histamine, so that allergies are rare among them—though cured schizophrenics are as susceptible to allergies as the rest of the population. They are also unlikely to develop rheumatoid arthritis or diabetes. Many have a great capacity for sustaining injury and life-threatening trauma without being immobilized. Non-schizophrenic relatives of schizophrenics, with presumably similar genetic makeups, have been found to be less susceptible than normal to viral infections, allergies and accidents.

Why Does It Strike?

Is schizophrenia the same for everybody—that is, caused by the same processes?

For most of the past two centuries schizophrenia has been considered to be one disease. For the past decade it has been revealed to be a number of syndromes, *i.e.*, there are a number of causes which yield diseases with similar symptoms—it is a brain dysfunction syndrome. In the same way, the pneumonia syndrome is caused by any infection in the lung: bacterial, viral, tubercular, and others. The schizophrenic syndrome is characterized by the presence of perceptual disturbances and thought disorder. This suggests there is a final common pathway no matter what the precipitating causes, a common fault in brain biochemistry which disturbs common areas of brain function.

Schizophrenia is both genetic and environmental.

Genetic? Most psychiatric books I've looked at call schizophrenia a psychological disease.

There is no doubt that something is passed on from one or both parents which increases the susceptibility to schizophrenia. If one member of a family has schizophrenia, the probability it will be present in any other member of that family depends upon the genetic similarity. Identical twins are as genetically close as any humans can be because they originate from a single fertilized egg which splits and creates two individuals. If one member of such a pair becomes schizophrenic, the odds it will attack the other are better than 50 percent. There may be a higher association if one takes into account response to vitamin therapy. I have records on fourteen pairs of twins, many of whom I treated. One member of one pair was schizophrenic, his identical twin brother was "normal." When the "normal" brother saw how well his sick brother became on vitamin treatment he also started to take the same vitamins. To his surprise he was much better in a month. They were both identical, but not quite. The normal brother had a slight need for extra vitamins, not enough to make him sick but enough to keep him from full health. The sick brother had a much greater vitamin dependency. Because schizophrenia is a clinical diagnosis, it will never be precise enough to allow anyone to determine the exact inheritance.

First order relatives (siblings, parents, children) have a probability of about 10 percent of developing schizophrenia, second order relatives (cousins) only have a 2 percent probability.

Identical twins whether raised together or in separate families still have the same high probability, about 50 percent.

Even when genetic factors for schizophrenia are present, this does not mean it must express itself. The same proportion of our population must have had the genes for schizophrenia before 1800, yet it was then a rare disease. It only began to appear in substantial numbers after 1800.

The genes for schizophrenia require the correct biochemical environment. As I see it, a gene for schizophrenia requires certain nutrients in above-average quantities. If it requires Vitamin B3, and if extra amounts of B3 are provided in time, the disease will not appear. These types of environmental factors determine whether or not the disease will appear.

What part does the environment play?

There are a number of environments, biochemical and psychosocial. Psychosocial factors include all those influences which shape a person. For many years these psychosocial variables were considered the main etiological causes. The height of the movement came about 1960, when psychoanalysts felt they had destroyed all genetic biochemical theories. Today, very few serious students of schizophrenia pay much attention to these factors, but they may play a role as stress factors. There are no schizophrenogenic mothers, or fathers, or grandmothers, or uncles, or aunts; these were all figments of the fertile imagination of psychoanalysts. But there are thoughtless, or hostile, or even evil parents who subject their children to tremendous stress. This will have an effect in increasing the probability that schizophrenia will appear.

What do you mean by stress?

It is hard to define stress, for what may be stressful to some is merely exhilarating to others. Most people know what is stressful to them. I will accept as stressful to people any factor which, continued long enough, threatens that person's health and life. It does not include getting up in the morning as some have defined it. Stress includes infections, trauma, surgery, pain, fear, exhaustion, overwork, too little rest, depression, intoxication, incarceration, grief, brutality. Perhaps one could define it as anything which alerts the fight-or-flight mechanisms or which decreases the amount of ascorbic acid in the adrenal medulla. Stress also includes utilization of ascorbic acid and its conversion to oxidized ascorbic acid. It changes the ratio. Normally not more than 7 percent of the ascorbic acid in blood is oxidized. Under stress much more is oxidized. The greater the stress, the higher the percentage. Life-threatening stress increases it to very high levels.

One common factor in all stress reactions is an increased utilization of, and therefore increased need for, water-soluble nutrients. The best examples are ascorbic acid for vitamins and zinc for minerals. If, therefore, the levels of nutrients are marginal, these people will be more readily thrown into a deficiency state by stress. If this is combined with malnutrition, the effect will be even greater. A person possessing genes which increase the need for nutrients will be more susceptible to stress.

Is a virus disease stressful for schizophrenics?

I have seen many patients who were getting on well but then

relapsed after a severe attack of influenza or hepatitis or some other illness. It requires several months for them to regain their previous state of health. This is one reason I place so many of my patients on ascorbic acid. It decreases the probability of getting an infection, and if it does strike they are able to withstand it better. The stress of being in hospital has been a major factor in initiating chronic illness. I have seen a large number of patients with chronic fatigue, tension and depression who date the onset of their illness from a prolonged stay in hospital following surgery. The stress of the illness, of the surgery, combined with the poor nutrition provided by the hospital is sufficient to throw many people into a chronic illness. They were probably marginal with respect to nutrients before admission. These patients recover when their diets are corrected and they are supplemented with the necessary vitamins.

If stress is not the main cause, does it play a role?

Stress is not a main cause of schizophrenia, but it can certainly be a contributing factor and must be taken into account.

It is vital when dealing with stress not to confuse cause and effect, for once an illness is present it generates a tremendous amount of stress. It may be like a positive feedback system; any upredictable bizarre behavior is very difficult to cope with and generates counterbehavior. Imagine the stress which develops between husband and wife if the husband becomes paranoid and wrongly suspects his wife is having an affair and accuses her of it. Recently I treated a woman who was convinced her husband was brutal, could not manage their business affairs and so on. Yet the husband had none of these characteristics. After she recovered, she realized these had been delusions and went back home. There has been no problem since. The degree of stress in that household had been great, leading to her running away from home to move into a motel and then being brought to our emergency unit by police. Often the family stress generated by the illness is so severe the patient must be removed by admission to hospital. One of the advantages of tranquilizers is that they reduce the level of bizarre, unusual and inappropriate behavior and reduce the level of stress.

If heredity and environment—what you're born with and what happens to you—don't fully account for schizophrenia, what's left?

Though both genetics and environment do play a role, one modifying the other, there are a number of other primary factors. They are primary because they lead to specific treatment. It is not possible to change our genetics and difficult to alter our environment. But when these primary causal factors are identified it becomes easier to follow a rational treatment plan.

There are a large number of primary causes; more are yet to be recognized. Those recognized so far are cerebral allergies, vitamin deficiencies and dependencies, mineral deficiencies and dependencies, amino acid problems, imbalances in unsaturated essential fatty acids, drug-induced reactions, brain damage, and chronic intoxication.

I'm familiar with allergies like hay fever and hives, but what are cerebral allergies?

This schizophrenic syndrome is caused by reactions to foods, or drugs or other chemicals present in our environment. The syndrome cannot be distinguished from other schizophrenic syndromes on clinical grounds, but it may have a different developmental history and respond differently to treatment. The first three schizophrenic patients I fasted for four days were well on the fifth day. One was allergic to aspirin, one was allergic to cigarettes and the last was allergic to certain foods.

Patients of this type will not recover until the allergies are recognized and dealt with or until a change in diet, which may be accidental, removes the offending foods. For this reason they tend to become chronic and eventually make up a major proportion of the chronic pool.

Vitamin treatment of the type I shall discuss later will not make these patients well. This is the reason why a few psychiatrists treating chronic patients have not seen any response to vitamin therapy. In the same way, a patient suffering a viral pneumonia will not recover on penicillin, but penicillin will cure a bacterial pneumonia.

Many years ago, Dr. Theron Randolph reported to an international congress of psychiatrists that a large proportion of psychiatric patients recovered when the allergies were identified and treated. He was ignored. About thirteen years ago, Dr. William Philpott at a joint meeting of the American Schizophrenia Association and the British Schizophrenia Association held in London reported that over 60 percent of schizophrenics were allergic to wheat and milk. This was an astonishing report, as standard teaching was that schizophrenics do not have any allergies.

Dr. Philpott had been introduced to the allergy concepts by Dr. Marshall Mandell. They later presented reports and films to the annual meetings of the Academy of Orthomolecular Psychiatry, the Huxley Institute for Biosocial Research and the Canadian Schizophrenia Foundation. Following this, I began to apply the principles developed by these medical scientists. It only took a few weeks of clinical investigation to confirm their findings. During the following two years I fasted about 160 schizophrenic patients. They had previously not responded to vitamins or tranquilizers, or had not responded well enough. After a four-day fast, over 100 had lost all schizophrenic symptoms. After that foods were tested individually to identify the ones they were allergic to. They are usually the staple foods: wheat, milk, sugar, corn, eggs and so on.

Physicians, patients and their families who have seen dramatic recoveries following a fast or other elimination diets do not doubt the concept of cerebral allergies. Physicians are skeptical when they hear or read about this, but the evidence is overwhelming. There are two lines of evidence, the recovery which follows removal of the offending foods or other substances, and the return of the schizophrenia following the reintroduction of those foods.

I have seen patients recover in a few days following a fast or in a few weeks following a simple elimination diet. Every physician using similar techniques has seen similar dramatic results. I have seen equally dramatic relapses following consumption of the offending foods. I have seen a patient start a meal friendly and at ease and gradually become more and more hostile and paranoid during its course. Another patient ate one chocolate bar and became psychotic and aggressive for four days.

I have never heard of vitamin dependencies. How do they differ from deficiencies?

Pellagra is the best example of a vitamin deficiency schizophrenia syndrome. It is caused by vitamin B3-deficient diets and also, in rarer cases, by pyridoxine deficiency. Pellagra is caused by a monotonous corn diet with very little meat, vegetables or other foods. Corn is deficient in vitamin B3 because it is bound so firmly to other constituents of the corn. It is also deficient in tryptophan, Omega-3 essential fatty acids and isoleucine. It also contains too much leucine.

Vitamin dependencies have been discussed. They are essentially no different than pellagra but the people are sick for different reasons.

With both deficiencies and dependencies the problem at the cellular level is the same: not enough nicotinamide adenine dinucleotide (NAD) is formed, so that there is too little of it within the cells and respiration is inhibited. NAD is a vital element of cell respiration.

Every physician is familiar with the concept of deficiency. Few are familiar with that of dependency. They find it difficult to accept that not everyone is the same and that some will need large quantities of any nutrient compared to others.

Are there any mineral dependencies?

The concept that mineral deficiencies and dependencies can cause a schizophrenic syndrome is so new that no surveys have been done to determine what proportion of any population belong to this group. Carl Pfeiffer and his colleagues have been most active in studying the relationship of minerals to schizophrenia.

Health food stores are making amino acids available. Do you approve?

The relationship between amino acids and schizophrenia has not been investigated very much. Pellagra is a multiple deficiency of both tryptophan and vitamin B3. It is likely that the skin changes characteristic of pellagra are due to tryptophan deficiency. Tryptophan dependency has not been described.

The ratio of isoleucine to leucine plays a role in pellagra and may play a role in schizophrenia.

The other amino acids will one day be examined as they relate to schizophrenia.

I have heard that linseed oil and evening primrose oil are helpful.

The ratio of omega-3 to omega-6 essential fatty acids plays a role. Dr. Donald Rudin has described what he calls "substrate pellagra." The essential fatty acids are converted into prostaglandins. These ubiquitous chemicals are involved in nearly every process in the body. It would not be surprising, therefore, that they play a role in schizophrenia as has been suggested by Drs. Donald Rudin and David Horrobin.

One of my friends is playing around with LSD. Can it make him schizophrenic?

A large number of drugs will cause a schizophrenic syndrome. The best known are the hallucinogens such as mescalin, peyote and LSD. Amphetamines will cause similar reactions as will related compounds. But it can also be caused by atropine and some anesthetics. These syndromes are usually short-lived, lasting only a few days. They are diagnosed by a history of drug abuse and by their rapid response to treatment.

What about alcohol and other drugs?

An intoxication is characterized by disorientation, memory disturbances and confusion, but it is not always possible to make a clear differentiation. This includes intoxication by drugs such as bromide (rarely used), alcohol and amphetamines (speed).

How do you put all these ideas together?

Schizophrenia will attack an individual who is genetically vulnerable, who is not aware of this vulnerability and does not alter the biochemical environment to meet the demands of his/her genetic inheritance. The genetic vulnerability may create a demand for more vitamins, or may make it more difficult to cope with allergens, or chemicals. There are probably two main sets of genes; one controls the final common pathway, which is why all the schizophrenic syndromes are similar, and the other set has to do with the specific syndromes already described.

My associate Humphry Osmond and I have developed a hypothesis about the genetic involvement in the final common pathway: that a genetic abnormality in schizophrenics brings about an excessive conversion of adrenalin to a substance called adrenochrome, which is a hallucinogen and is also capable of producing some of the significant physical characteristics associated with schizophrenia, such as increased pigmentation of hair and skin, decreased incidence of arthritis, low temperature and disturbed carbohydrate metabolism.

Our work indicates very strongly that this hypothesis accounts for the clinical, biochemical and physiological findings in schizophrenia. This is borne out by the fact that the hypothesis suggests that vitamin B3 and ascorbic acid, which are adrenochrome antagonists, would be effective in treating the schizophrenia syndrome; and this is actually the case.

The Impact

Schizophrenia has a tremendous impact on individuals and their families, doesn't it?

Schizophrenia is a variable disease. Its impact on the patient ranges from having hardly any effect to complete destruction of life. Any disease which attacks the brain can have a profound impact, but there are many variables involved in determining the outcome, and the disease itself may for some patients be a minor factor. Patients will have the best prognosis when each treatment factor operates at the maximum therapeutic level.

Why are so many patients who behave badly refused the diagnosis of schizophrenia? Isn't that disastrous?

The Medical Model—treating the condition as a disease—is the only model which provides for all the factors essential to treat patients, because it mobilizes the psychiatric, nursing and community support resources better than any other model. A patient who has committed an antisocial (criminal) act and is charged may be dealt with in several ways such as being treated while charges are dropped, or being declared not mentally ill and proceeding through the criminal justice system, or by a combination of both. The future of the patient will depend on the path followed.

The criminal justice system may suspect that the person is ill and will then seek a psychiatric opinion. Often patients are remanded to a psychiatric ward for observation designed to lead to accurate diagnosis. The wrong decision may destroy that individual. This is illustrated by the following history of a teenage girl who had twice set fire to her home, had been remanded to a forensic ward for examination and had been diagnosed not mentally ill. She was therefore blacklisted by every psychiatric unit in Vancouver, British Columbia. They had concluded she should be dealt with by the criminal justice system. Dr. Thomas Szasz would have approved of their decision, for he is determined that there are no mentally sick people, that anyone who commits a crime must be dealt with as a criminal. This decision left the judge who had to deal with this girl in a very difficult position. He had apparently concluded she was ill and did not want to send her to prison. The parents were desperate for help but could not take her home because her behavior was so unpredictable. Finally both parents consulted me on a Wednesday. I agreed to see her as an emergency two days later. Meanwhile she was being held in a prison cell in Vancouver.

Her parents informed the judge I had agreed to see her, and may have added I would admit her to hospital in Victoria. The judge promptly released her to her parents and dropped the charges on the condition she was seen by me. When I examined her I found a very psychotic young girl, so ill I could have been charged with malpractice had I not admitted her immediately to hospital as an emergency. She is now nearly normal. Here is her story, obtained September 11, 1981.

Jean, born in 1963, had been nervous most of her life. By the age of three she was hyperactive. Later she developed learning problems and required special tutoring for math and social studies. At age fourteen she developed fears and phobias, became disoriented and began to binge on junk food, gaining twenty pounds in one month. After that she would gain and lose weight. At about fifteen she was treated in a university psychiatric hospital for four months and from there was transferred to a home for disturbed adolescents for one and one-half years. At seventeen she was made a ward of the government. By the end of 1980 she was found unmanageable in a group home. She was then in grade 9. From there she was admitted to a local psychiatric ward for two weeks then returned home. In January 1981 she set fire to her mattress because she was angry at the world. She was readmitted for a few days and later seen as a day patient. During this interval she made three suicide attempts. Later in the year she set fire to the curtains of her bedroom. She was admitted that year to a large mental hospital for two months and was found *mentally normal.* After her second fire no hospital would admit her and she was taken by the R.C.M.P. to Oakalla prison for a week. When I saw her she presented the following mental state.

Perception: She had suffered visual hallucinations from the age of fifteen, seeing people with knives. She also heard voices ordering her to do bad things which had told her to set the fires. She heard her own thoughts and felt weird.
Thought: She was very paranoid, believing people were talking about her, plotting against her and watching her. There was blocking. Her concentration was poor.
Mood: She was depressed and tired.
Behavior: Inappropriate.

She was clearly schizophrenic, yet after two months in a mental hospital she was declared to be mentally normal!

I admitted her to hospital and started a long, comprehensive treatment program. By November 14, 1984, she was becoming more and more mature and dependable, and was on her way to completing high school. Earlier with her family she had been a tourist in Europe for about six weeks. Had she been denied the Medical Model she would now be in prison or in a chronic mental hospital ward. The psychiatrists who declared her normal, and by inference criminal, would have destroyed her.

So using the wrong model can be very harmful?

The public is not protected by avoiding the Medical Model. Too often patients are diagnosed using a legal definition. In December 1984, in Stillwater, Minnesota, Michael Babo was charged with murder. His mother had tried unsuccessfully to have him committed to a mental hospital for she feared he would harm someone. He was released after three days of observation at St. Paul Ramsay Medical Center. He did not meet the legal requirements to be labelled mentally ill, even though he was considered a danger to the public— hostile and suspicious, with limited intelligence. The day after his discharge the burned body of his mother was found in her room by firefighters. Michael Babo may not have been *legally* mentally ill, but he certainly *was* mentally ill—probably schizophrenic.

I imagine age plays a most important role in shaping schizophrenia?

Obviously, the earlier the disease strikes the more devastating are the consequences if no treatment or inappropriate treatment is given. Maturation follows an inexorable pattern. Babies learn to move, walk, run, jump, speak, control their bladder and bowel within a narrow time frame. If the child is not walking well by the age of two, this may become a permanent problem. The brain is most plastic early in infancy for all these human activities which provide the basis for mature life. If the child is still not speaking by age five it may never speak. Social skills are also learned over a certain time frame. Learning how to interact with other children begins early in life and the basis for one's future interactions is probably pretty well established by puberty. Education has to be obtained over a critical period. If a person can not read by the time he is ten, it may always be difficult thereafter. This applies to people who had an opportunity to learn to read. Dyslexia carried on into adulthood permanently makes reading very difficult.

Schizophrenia distorts perception, creates problems in thinking and interferes with the normal development pattern. Its impact is greatest in people who have not yet matured; infants will not learn how to speak, and will not learn how to interact appropriately with their parents, brothers and sisters, or others. The effect on the individual will be determined by the nature of the perceptual changes and their intensity. If words on a page are mobile, move back and forth, fade and come back, it will be very difficult to learn to read. This is what dyslexia is. Dyslexics prefer to learn by hearing rather than by reading. This is how intelligent dyslexic children and adults can be so successful and often can cover their reading disability so no one is aware of it.

Another important factor is the proportion of the time of each phase occupied by the illness. If an infant suffers from a severe milk allergy causing dyslexia and behavioral problems (usually hyperactivity) for a year and then is placed on a milk-free diet, that child should catch up on its normal development by the it is ready for school. If the allergy is not treated for five years, it will be much more difficult for the child to join its peers in normal development, but it can still happen. Schizophrenia which develops after age three, when speech, motor activity and social behavior are reasonably well developed, has a much better prognosis compared to schizophrenic children who are stricken earlier.

A six-year-old boy was brought to me by his father, a physician. Both parents were very concerned over his behavior. A few months before, he had torn the antenna (rabbit ears) off a TV set, and when asked why, reported that he had seen God, who had told him to. Later, he began to talk about seeing many things in the shadows, sometimes during the day, and in his nightmares. He could not sleep without a night light. He was also hyperactive. A female cousin on his mother's side was ill, and I had started her on a vitamin program more than twelve years before. She followed her program and became and remains normal. An uncle on the mother's side was schizophrenic but could not follow my program. He is still ill, getting by on tranquilizers. The physician father was very worried that his son was also schizophrenic. He obtained information from the Canadian Schizophrenia Foundation about vitamins and doses, and, two months before I saw him, had started the program. When I saw the boy, he was almost well, with no further hallucinations or illusions, and he was not hyperactive.

An adolescent who becomes sick at puberty is plucked out of the mainstream of life whether or not she or he is treated in hospital. Peers continue to mature, become educated and develop more social skills while the sick teenager is denied these opportunities. Diseases tend to center one's attention on oneself, but schizophrenia creates more self-centeredness than most other diseases. After it has been present a long time, the patient may be so self-centered it is impossible to live with him.

Adolescent patients, even when they recover, have to work hard to overcome the psychosocial disabilities forced on them by their illness. The best time to become schizophrenic, if it is bound to come, is late in life when it does the least damage. A few elderly schizophrenics may, in fact, never be diagnosed. They will be accepted as ecccentrics or as having unusual quirks: Aunt Mary may become very suspicious when she has a drink and Uncle Tom may talk to himself when no one is around. A few seniles are, in fact, elderly schizophrenics and are not devastated by the illness.

Schizophrenia during adulthood will do little harm when treated promptly and efficiently. Some even benefit from a short, strange interlude which shows them a world they may have seen only in their dreams, but a prolonged illness benefits no one, no matter what R. D. Laing and his disciples may say. I have yet, having seen thousands of schizophrenics in thirty-five years, to find one who enjoyed it and wanted to return to that strange world. I have not found any who resolved any major conflicts as a result of having been ill. It always creates many problems which must be solved.

Schizophrenia generally makes it impossible for people to live up to their psychosocial potential. Schizophrenic sons and daughters of productive, creative people when untreated are not able to match their parents' creativity and productivity. The main determinants of the impact of schizophrenia are the age at which it first strikes and the duration of the illness. This means that treatment must be started early, using the best treatment program available, and it should be anticipated long before it occurs. Recently, Meillon and Reading (1984), in a most important book, disclose how a medical genealogy can be used to predict the probability that schizophrenia will appear. The population may be divided into those where there is no history of schizophrenia in any member of the family for as many generations as there is information and into families where there is a history of schizophrenia or something like it. With the second group the likelihood of being hit depends upon the genetic similarity to members of the family known to have been ill. Identical twins have the highest probability, while distant cousins have the least probability. This will be elaborated in the section dealing with the inheritance of schizophrenia.

Individuals who are vulnerable should see to it that their lifestyle and nutrition will prevent the schizophrenia from appearing. Families where one parent has been ill should ensure that their children avoid junk food and excessive quantities of cereals and milk. If there are early worrisome changes in behavior or learning ability, they should promptly eliminate foods containing added sugar and other additives, check for the presence of food allergies and use vitamin supplements when these measures are not in themelves adequate.

Relatives should suspect schizophrenia in those who suffer from excessive fatigue and mood disorders not attributable to other conditions. Even if they are apparently well, it is worth determining whether improving their diet, and if necessary adding supplements, might make them even better. I had a schizophrenic man who recovered. When his identical twin brother, a teacher, saw the remarkable change in his brother, he placed himself on a similar program. Even though he had not considered himself ill, he was surprised at how much better he was after starting on his brother's program.

Is there a danger that the schizophrenic patient will try to commit suicide?

Classically, suicide is associated with depression, especially depression which lasts a long time, but it is also common in schizophrenia and any other condition or disease when all hope is lost. The cardinal symptoms one must watch for are depression and, even more, loss of hope. I routinely ask every depressed patient about suicide. It is reassuring for them to be able to discuss these thoughts and to know that depression is often associated with the idea of suicide. Knowing that the depression will leave is the best antidote to suicide. When it is not possible to convince patients things will get better, they should be admitted to hospital and watched very carefully for the first few days until the depression begins to lift.

Intoxication, particularly with alcohol or with hallucinogenic drugs, may create moments of hopelessness during which a suicide attempt is made. Many patients are seen in hospital emergency departments for treatment of a suicide attempt, usually an overdose, after drinking too much. Usually they are over this in a day or two and seldom remain suicidal.

I have heard that one-third of schizophrenics will recover without any treatment. Is that true?

Schizophrenia may attack and then may remit. Students of schizophrenia believe that one-third of acute (early) cases will recove spontaneously, without treatment. I no longer believe that this is true. The proportion who recover spontaneously is probably much less, perhaps around ten percent. The one-third recovery statistic was obtained many years ago from hospitalized patients. If a patient no longer needed to be readmitted, he was considered recovered. Yet I have seen many patients who had only one admission but thereafter continued to suffer from depression, irritability and fatigue, with slight distortion of their personality. They were able to get by but were not well. When they were started on nutritional treatment, they did recover and were freed of their debilitating symptoms. I am not even sure whether the ten percent who do recover do so spontaneously. Perhaps they have intuitively discovered which foods to avoid, thus eliminating foods they were allergic to. I know one family which achieved such a "spontaneous" recovery. The patient's mother noted that after certain foods her son's behavior became much worse. She eliminated this food from his diet and he began to recover. Dr. C. Pfeiffer described a family whose daughter was very aggressive and psychotic. She had not responded to any treatment including tranquilizers or vitamins. Her family observed that after a meal of oysters she became well for a few days. Oysters are very rich in zinc. Placing her on zinc supplementation maintained her health. Her "spontaneous" recovery followed the addition of a food item to her diet.

Discontinuous schizophrenia is that form of the disease which oscillates between severe psychosis and normality, or at least some improvement. The disease in these patients has not caused permanent damage. If a patient can be normal for even one hour, there are grounds for optimism, since there has been no brain damage. These patients have shown a capacity to recover. The prognosis for discontinuous schizophrenia is better than for the continuous, unremitting type. Also, the impact on the patient is less severe.

Many psychiatrists would not diagnose schizophrenia if it were discontinuous. A few psychiatrists reserve the diagnosis only for those who had shown no improvement for at least fourteen years. Any patient who recovered was rediagnosed as having some other disease.

Continuous schizophrenia may be a different variety, with an element of brain damage in some. Their prognosis is not nearly as good, but this pessimistic conclusion may be wrong. Many of these continuous schizophrenics are examples of cerebral allergies. If they are allergic to wheat, for example, which causes their psychosis, they will remain ill until the wheat is eliminated. I have seen chronic schizophrenics become normal after a four-day water fast. But if the schizophrenia is present too long, the psychosocial consequences may have been so damaging that treatment becomes extremely difficult and slow.

Why are so many families excluded from the treatment program?

Schizophrenic patients, more than most other types, need strong family support; yet, because of the distortion in personality and lack of insight in many, it is one of the most difficult conditions to support. Often they are so sick they can not be left in the family and must be treated in hospital. If families are forced to restructure their lives, to convert their homes into mini-hospitals, there is a limit to their ability to cope. Patients may then need to be admitted to hospital for their own sake but also to give the family a chance to recuperate in preparation for continuing treatment.

Without family support, it becomes much harder to treat and the prognosis is much worse unless an alternate home can be found which provides equivalent care. Patients may do better in such a home because they cannot fall back into the old pathological parent/ child relationship generated by the disease. Also, one or both parents may have milder expressions of schizophrenia, which may intensify the problem.

The mother's health is probably the most important factor. If she is on the edge of schizophrenia, she may find it too difficult to cope with a sick son or daughter. On the other hand, if the mother has been schizophrenic and is well, she will have more understanding of her child. Many years ago, I treated a young woman who was very disoriented and paranoid. She had slowly developed the belief Christ would come from the heavens and take her bodily back with Him to be His bride. In preparation for this she began to spend as much time as possible studying the Bible. She could no longer cope with her job as head stenographer in a very large company. She recovered on vitamin treatment. During one visit I sympathized with her mother. She replied that she was able to cope because, when she had been her daughter's age, she had gone through a similar experience. She understood her daughter's experience and had no difficulty caring for her and waiting patiently for her recovery.

Parents must become allies in the fight against schizophrenia. They must be fully informed about diagnosis, the causes, all the details of treatment and what to expect. I usually have parents in my office while I am discussing treatment with the patient and during follow-up visits. All the details of treatment are discussed thoroughly. This includes the diet, the nutrients and drugs, giving details of dose, side effects and so on.

Most families want to help their sick relative. Unfortunately, for several decades it was traditional for psychiatrists to alienate the family by not telling them anything, by blaming them and by developig a set in which patient and doctor were antagonistic to the family. This pernicious approach is rapidly losing ground as psychiatrists return to the Medical Model. Still, I continue to find patients and families who tell me how they were blamed.

Up to fifteen years ago when I told mothers of schizophrenic children they had not created the illness, many would burst into tears—they had been blamed for this so often, they expected another series of unpleasant encounters with another psychiatrist. It is an important part of the Medical Model not to blame anyone for having caused the disease.

When I was diagnosed and started on your treatment, my family doctor and social worker made fun of your use of vitamins and nutrition. Isn't it important to have the community's resources behind one?

Community support is important to enhance the patient's probability of getting well. With any new treatment, the main obstacle to it is the medical profession and, next, social workers. With standard treatment, using only tranquilizers, there is much better medical support. General practitioners are familiar with tranquilizers and their side effects and will encourage their patients to continue with treatment. Nor will they be criticized by their colleagues. They do not have to accept the responsibility for the patient's failure to recover, since that is what they expect.

When patients are started on a nutrition/supplement program, GPs are immediately confronted by a new situation. They have been taught in medical school that vitamins are not needed, that the average diet is adequate, and that vitamins in large doses are dangerous, or at least wasteful. When they discover what their patients are taking, they will at best cooperate by not saying anything bad about the program, but they may also criticize the program and discourage the patient from continuing it. The usual support system available to patients on tranquilizers only is usually not available to patients receiving vitamins.

Many treatment failures are directly attributable to GPs who interfered in the treatment program. Here is one case which illustrates this point.

Many years ago I saw an epileptic schizophrenic who had also been an alcoholic. While drunk, he had shot a policeman and had been given a prison sentence which he served in Ontario in a prison institution. After discharged he drifted across Canada to Vancouver, where he was helped to stop drinking by the Salvation Army. He came back east through Saskatoon, where he was seen and referred to me. On examination he was very psychotic. His main delusion was that the Mafia was after him. His epilepsy was controlled by anticonvulsant medication. He was started on niacin and over a few months recovered and was able to find a job. Later on he went to Calgary. While in Calgary he saw a physician for a physical problem and told him the vitamins he was using. That physician promptly ordered him to stop using that dangerous material, insisting it was of no value and was dangerous. Within a few months the patient had relapsed and his convulsions were worse. At last he realized he must start treatment again, came to Saskatoon to see me and I restarted his vitamin program.

Many patients have to battle their physicians who are cynical or hostile until the patient changes doctors or decides not to tell them they are taking vitamins. I have seen many patients who recovered, letting their physicians believe it was the drug they had given them which was responsible when that drug, after an adequate trial, had done nothing.

The medical support system tries to destroy the nutritional program even in hospital. It is not unusual for patients to be admitted to hospital several times between the time treatment is started and the time they are well. With treatment with tranquilizers only, this is expected. If such a patient is admitted, the tranquilizer he is on may be changed, but only to be replaced by another. The treating psychiatrist does not denigrate the treatment and persuade the patient not to use it. One tranquilizer replaces another, but the basic treatment remains the same. When patients of mine are admitted to hospital, the psychiatrists promptly sequester all their nutrients and spend some time persuading the patients they do them no good. In one case the chief surgeon had a fight with one of my patients. The patient and her mother listened to him and then fired him. If they stay in hospital long enough, they may relapse back to their original state and when they are discharged have to start all over again. Each hospitalization brings about a short-term improvement because they have been heavily tranquilized, but at the cost of long-term harm and prolonged treatment.

Nursing staff must also be part of the support system. If staff is aware of the role nutrients play, they will ensure that the medication orders are followed. I have never had a problem with my patients, but other physicians have. One physician, under investigation for using vitamins, had to respond to a nurse at a hearing who told them he was giving his patients vitamins which made them turn red (the niacin flush). This statement achieved headlines in the local paper. Another nurse reported to her chief that a psychiatrist was using vitamins, and this was reported to a state board. The board advised the hospital that it would lose its license. That hospital, which had been grateful to the psychiatrist because of the business he generated, removed him from staff. Soon they negated this action and tried to get him back. He would not return, and practiced happily somewhere else.

Hospital nutritionists and dietitians must also cooperate. In October 1984 I admitted a young female schizophrenic and ordered a sugar-free diet and vitamins, including vitamin C. I had not had any difficulty in this good hospital in over eight years of practice there. This time, since I had ordered a special diet, the dietitian spoke to my patient. She saw on the order sheet that she was on vitamin C. She advised my patient that this was dangerous and might cause kidney stones. My patient became very disturbed and spoke to her general practitioner, who reassured her I knew more about vitamins than the dietitian. But my patient remained anxious, and I had to visit her after work to reassure her. However, she wanted to be discharged, stating she could no longer trust a hospital which gave her bad advice. As she was much better by then, I discharged her. With a traditional medical practice this kind of sabotage of a treatment does not occur, at least not by professional staff.

Don't schizophrenic patients need special education?

The educational system has little bias against patients, provided they conduct themselves as do other students. But schizophrenics who have been sick a long time have special requirements which the educational system should not have to provide. They have to be taught all those matters which they would have learned had they not become sick, such as how to dress appropriately, how to relate to people, how to apply for things such as jobs and theater tickets, how to eat in public, how to shop. These are essentials if the patient is to become a useful member of society. Once they have mastered these, they can learn whatever else they need to learn in the community.

They also need job training either on the the job or by taking courses.

What kind of homes should patients have?

One of the reasons that the massive discharge program from mental hospitals failed was that inadequate provisions were made for discharged patients. They were all on tranquilizers, and psychiatrists were unaware that it was very difficult for these patients to fend for themselves, to find homes and to conduct the routine business of living. If psychiatrists were taking tranquilizers and were asked to do the same, they would soon realize these difficulties. Just because patients no longer hallucinate does not mean they are fit to live alone.

The usual move is from hospital to home, for patients who have a home. This is the ideal situation, but consideration must be given to the impact on the home. It must not be overlooked or the entire family may disintegrate. A warm, supportive home environment is ideal. It must not be a mini-hospital. If the patient is so sick that a hospital environment is needed, he ought to remain in hospital.

Many patients require transitional homes. A hospital may discharge a patient to a sheltered or group home. These are private homes managed by personnel working for nonprofit institutions or for themselves. The quality of care varies with the skill and energy of the manager. A few of my patients live in these homes and they are given superb care. They may live there forever, but my objective is to use these homes as preparation for independent living. When they have improved even more, they may move into their own supervised and subsidised apartments. This is cheaper than keeping them in hospital. From these homes some are ready to seek work, to take jobs and to begin life in the community.

My illness has cost me a good deal of money—is that a widespread problem?

The economic cost of schizophrenia is enormous—hospital costs, medical costs, medication, legal fees, welfare payments, and loss of productivity. I have estimated that every teenage schizophrenic will cost the community about one million dollars, assuming he will survive another forty years and assuming a five percent annual inflation factor. Every schizophrenic treated successfully saves the the community the same amount. Since very few patients treated by orthodox psychiatry ever recover, while most of those treated by orthomolecular psychiatry do, the cost difference between the two treatment modes is enormous.

If the community and its leaders, government especially, were really serious about cutting health costs, they could do so very quickly by providing all their schizophrenic patients with optimum treatment.

Would you list for me the factors which either help or hinder recovery?

All factors which promote recovery and health will reduce the deleterious impact of the disease on the patient. Conversely, all negative factors will increase the impact and decrease the probability of recovery. These are shown in the following table. Positive factors, in my view, are, in order of descending significance, orthomolecular treatment, use of the Medical Model, availability of good hospitals, family support, community support, onset of the disease after puberty, and discontinuity of the illness. The negative factors, predictably, are the opposites: treatment by tranquilizers only, use of legal, psychiatric or other models, poor hospitals, lack of family and community support, prepubertal onset, and continuous illness.

The Treatment Program and Its Background

Once it's established that someone has schizophrenia and he accepts it, what next? How is it treated?

There are a variety of treatment programs, ranging from psychoactive drugs to psychotherapy, often combining them, sometimes with the use of electroconvulsive therapy, ECT. The results are mixed, with psychotherapy alone apparently the least valuable.

In my own experience, the program Dr. Humphry Osmond and I helped to develop has been effective in about 85 percent of cases of schizophrenia, both mild and severe. As this is a good deal more effective than results demonstrated by other programs, I will describe it briefly.

This program is one of what I call orthomolecular psychiatry. "Orthomolecular" is a term devised by Dr. Linus Pauling in 1968, referring to restoring a "right molecule" balance to the body by supplying it with appropriate amounts of nutrients—vitamins, minerals and so on. Theory indicates, and experience has borne out, that this very often results in righting the chemical imbalance in the brain which produces the schizophrenic symptoms.

Our program uses the other treatments in use today, such as tranquilizers, antidepressants, ECT and so on, but they take second place to the nutrient therapy.

The basic nutrient medicine is vitamin B3, in the form either of niacin or niacinamide. Niacin causes a flushing, tingling sensation in most patients, but most don't find it too uncomfortable; if they do, niacinamide, which does not cause that reaction, can be used. One advantage of niacin is that it lowers blood cholesterol.

For patients who have been ill a short time and are able to cooperate in their treatment in their own home, we start with a dose of three grams a day. If improvement is shown in one to three months, we advise keeping on at the same dosage level for five years. After that it can be stopped for a time and discontinued entirely if the symptoms don't recur.

And if the patient doesn't show signs of getting better in three months?

We increase the dose, usually in increments of three grams, until we get a proper response or until side effects appear. The highest dose, which is very rare, is up to about 30 grams a day.

Is the B3 all you use?

No, we also employ ascorbic acid, vitamin C, starting with 3 grams a day. Stress uses up a lot of ascorbic acid in the body, and schizophrenia is a highly stressful condition. We are also now using pyridoxine, vitamin B6, especially with children. Vitamin B1, thiamine, can be useful in depression, with a dose range of anywhere from 100 to 3,000 milligrams a day; vitamin B12 combined with folic acid can also be helpful.

For some people other vitamins are advisable, depending on their condition. For instance, those with surface lesions on the skin or mucous membranes will be given vitamin A; older patients or those with circulatory problems will get vitamin E and often pantothenic acid.

And you use drugs at the same time?

To the extent that they are needed. The important thing is to give the optimum dose, one which relieves the disturbing symptoms without producing serious side effects or immobilizing the patient.

The objective is to get the patient to a point in his recovery at which he can be sustained by the nutrient therapy alone.

I should emphasize that the vitamins aren't enough by themselves; good nutrition in general is a necessity, for all of us and especially for the schizophrenic patient. One frequent symptom is weight loss, and we encourage our patients to put on weight if possible. That can sometimes lead to trouble if everybody involved does not understand what is going on; one of our patients got to be twenty pounds overweight, and her family doctor put her on an amphetamine reducing pill—a bad idea at best, but amphetamines are dangerous for schizophrenics, which he didn't know, and her symptoms returned.

That's what you do with people who can still be treated in the home. What about when they're worse, and have to be hospitalized?

In addition to the nutrient therapy, we employ a short course of electroconvulsive therapy on a very small percentage of hospitalized patients.

Shock treatment?

That is the popular name, and it is misleading. There is no shock, no pain, no drop in blood pressure. As soon as the current is applied in ECT, the patient falls into a deep sleep and then has a convulsive seizure of which he is completely unaware. There are usually fewer than ten treatments, sometimes as many as fifteen.

We give ECT with the consent of the patient except in rare cases, and even in those the patient recovered and was grateful that we had gone against his disordered will.

After the ECT series the patient is watched carefully for a week to ten days. If we see improvement, we recommend continuing the vitamin dosage for five years.

And if you don't see improvement then?

If that is the case, the odds are that the disease has been present so long that it has become chronic and treatment will have to go on for a long time, at home or in the hospital. The basic treatment remains the nutrient therapy, with sometimes occasional series of ECT.

Well, that's what you do, and apparently it works. But **why** does it work? The vitamins, for instance—you say that they restore the "right molecules" to the body or some such. But that doesn't really tell me much. If that's the core of the therapy, it would help me to know something about it in detail.

There is a lot of detail, and a lot of history, involved.

I'm here to learn.

Very well, then. After the discovery by Funk of vitamins and the great expansion of nutritional knowledge in the early part of this century, it was inevitable that vitamins, minerals and other nutrients would be used as therapeutic compounds in doses much larger than quantities found even in the best food. Soon after niacin and niacinamide were recognized to be vitamin B3, the anti-pellagra vitamin, they were being used in doses much larger than the Recommended Daily Allowance. These RDAs have a limited validity; they were established as a guide for people who were healthy, and have no bearing on patients. Since about one-half of the population may have one or more illnesses, and many have special needs, it is obvious that RDAs will not be of any help to clinical nutritionists who advise patients. Pellagrologists were soon giving patients up to 600 milligrams per day of vitamin B3. This is over one hundred times the RDA. They found that chronic pellagrins neeed this much before their symptoms began to abate. This puzzled them, as these large doses violated the definition of a vitamin. They also used these large doses for patients with deteriorating neurological diseases and confusional states.

When I began my literature search in 1951, I discovered that a few investigators had already reported on the use of 1½ gram (1500 mg) doses for psychiatric cases. Also, Dr. W. Kaufman had begun to use 4 grams per day in 1945 on a series of arthritics with great success. About the same time, Doctors W. Shute and E. Shute were caught in a vigorous medical controversy because they were using 1 gram per day and more of vitamin E, for the treatment of patients with cardiovascular disease. Dr. F. Klenner had been using very large doses of vitamin C, but there was no controversy here because no one had ever heard of his work. The vitamin C controversy began when Linus Pauling published his famous book, *Vitamin C and the Common Cold*. The use of large doses, incorrectly called megadoses, was a logical extension of what had started in the 1930s.

Larger doses were used because smaller doses had not worked. Every therapeutic drug or vitamin must be given in optimum doses. Drug companies determine the optimum dosage range of their compounds before they are released to the public. There is nothing mysterious about this. Ideally, the optimum dose does the job—is efficacious—without toxic or unpleasant side effects. The optimum dose relative to the toxic dose is called the therapeutic index. If the optimum dose is 10 mg per day and the toxic dose 1000 mg per day, the therapeutic index is 100. Clinicians and drug companies like compounds with a large index. If the most efficacious dose is 10 mg and the toxic dose is 20 mg, the index is 2. This would be a dangerous drug. But dangerous drugs may have to be used if nothing else is available. Insulin is relatively dangerous, but it is needed, and when used by intelligent, knowledgeable diabetics is safe.

The efficacious dose is the most important consideration. If a substance is considered efficacious it will be used no matter how dangerous it is, if nothing else is available. If a drug is not efficacious there is no point in taking it, no matter how safe it is. It is therefore pointless to argue about toxicity unless two equally efficacious compounds are available, then one must use the safer one.

Vitamins are unusually safe chemicals. For example, in dogs the LD 50 for vitamin B3, the amount which will kill half the test animals, is about 5 grams per kilogram of body weight. For a 50 kg human this is equivalent to 250 grams, or over one-half pound. No one knows what the LD 50 for people is, but assuming it is 250 grams per day, then the therapeutic index for 1 gram doses is 250. It is very safe.

Nevertheless, most physicians and nutritionists, hypnotized by the vitamin concept and RDAs, are strongly opposed to using large doses of vitamins. At least they are in public. Many are quietly using megadoses of vitamin E, megadoses of vitamin B12 and others. I will examine why there are so many bitter critics of megavitamin therapy. Then I will discuss why many patients will not get well until they are given large doses of some of the vitamins.

I have read that vitamins are needed only in very small doses. You obviously do not agree.

This is standard dogma based entirely on theoretical notions about vitamins. There is a vast and rapidly growing literature to the contrary. Even the FDA has approved megadoses of niacin for the treatment of cholesterol levels when they are too high—3 to 6 grams per day are required. Critics who claim that only minute doses are required must back up their claims with controlled research. They have no studies to support their claims; all they can point to are studies showing that small doses of vitamins will cure terminal diseases such as beri-beri, scurvy and pellagra. No one has ever claimed that megadoses are needed to keep people from dying of these diseases; the usual recommended doses will protect most people from these classical, pre-death diseases. We do not know how many, as studies have been done on very small samples. If people want better health than that, they may need much larger doses. The concept of vitamin deficiencies has had a very pernicious, harmful effect on our population.

My doctor tells me I may as well flush the vitamins down the toilet—that only the fish in the sea will benefit.

Cynics will tell their patients they will not be helped but that they will enrich their urine. These cynics are almost totally ignorant of vitamin physiology and biochemistry. It is correct that a proportion of water-soluble vitamins are excreted; in the same way, penicillin finds its way into the urine. A few very serious infections require many grams of antibiotics per day. Most appears in the urine, which is appropriately enriched with the antibiotics. Yet I have never heard any critic criticize anyone for using large amounts of antibiotics when they are required.

The more of a water-soluble vitamin one ingests, the more remains in the body. One must waste some in order to achieve the therapeutic effect.

Vitamins are needed in large amounts for many reasons. There may be a problem transporting them across membranes, *i.e.*, from gut to blood and from blood to cells. Only one-half of one percent of the vitamin C and niacin administered enters the brain. The blood/ brain barrier is very effective; from 3000 mg, only 15 mg enters the brain. There may be a problem in creating the enzyme of which the vitamin is a component. There may be too much of another enzyme which destroys vitamins. Perhaps one day we will be able to determine which particular factor increases the need for large doses. At the moment, it is sufficient to know that for many people only large doses of vitamins allow them to remain well.

My family doctor told me that these vitamins are harmful. Is that true?

Vitamins are in fact very safe—comparable to food in safety. They are safe because they are bulky, so it is difficult to take enormous amounts, they are water-soluble in most cases, so they do not build up in the body, and they are natural molecules life has been comfortable with for millions of years. The body does not need to develop new processes in order to deal with them. Fat-soluble vitamins can accumulate and are less safe, but even their toxicity has been grossly exaggerated. Toxicity has been ascribed to vitamins on the basis of faulty chemical analyses and extrapolations not warranted by the data. I will examine these in detail with each vitamin.

Does anyone else agree with you that vitamins are safe?

Dr. John Marks recently reviewed the safety of vitamins used in orthomolecular doses. The review is distributed by the Vitamin Information Service of Hoffman-La Roche. It contains information about thirteen vitamins and has a vitamin safety bibliography containing 117 papers. In his introduction Dr. Marks writes, "Sometimes the intake has assumed heroic levels. In consequence, cases of alleged adverse reactions to vitamins are reported periodically in the press with support ranging from the anecdotal to the scientific. These in turn are frequently reiterated by well-intentioned writers without any case details or adequate scientific report increasing the implied credibility."

After reviewing eleven papers and reviews Marks concludes:

1. "There is no satisfactory internationally accepted standard for advised intake of vitamins."
2. Levels of vitamins normally used by the majority of the general population are safe. The risk of adverse reactions appears to be greater when high doses are taken without professional advice.
3. "There is a considerable margin of safety with most of the vitamins."
4. "The safety margin is particularly true for water-soluble vitamins."
5. With the "exception of certain adverse reactions from ingested vitamins A and D, the rare cases of vitamin side effects that occur are rapidly reversible on withdrawal of the supplementation and leave minimal or usually no lasting effects."

Orthomolecular physicians and subjects using vitamins in large doses are interested particularly in pyridoxine, niacin and/or niacinamide, and ascorbic acid.

A review of twelve reports dealing with pyridoxine led to the conclusion that it was safe with doses under 2,000 mg per day. It does not cause liver damage, does not interfere with riboflavin activity, nor does it cause a dependency state.

A review of fifteen papers on vitamin B3 (not including any of mine) shows it to be safe. Marks wonders whether the flushing effect should in fact be considered an adverse reaction, since it is a natural reaction to niacin and is used therapeutically.

A further review of twenty-seven papers on vitamin C (not including any papers by I. Stone, L. Pauling, me, or any orthomolecular physicians) prove it is safe. Marks states, "Although the scientific evidence for these uses is increasing steadily, there are still critics of high-dose administration. They have alleged that the substance causes kidney stones, interference with vitamin B12 metabolism, rebound scurvy, excessive iron metabolism and has a mutagenic effect," but "an extensive and very thorough analysis of the data during the past years has disproved all serious allegations."

Marks lists the following RDAs and a ratio of High Safety/RDA.

Vitamin	RDA (mg)	Ratio
Pyridoxine	22	+
Vitamin B3	18	+
Vitamin C	60	+ +

+ Safety level 50 to 100 times RDA
+ + Safety level at least 100 times RDA

John Marks is rather conservative in his estimates, by a factor of two or three. Ascorbic acid has been used in doses much higher. I do agree that these high doses should be supervised by physicians who know the vitamins and what they can do.

Unfortunately, the vast majority of physicians will not read Marks's excellent review. I try to help a bit. *The Canadian Medical Association Journal* published a letter I had written, in which I refer to the medical literature showing that the original method for measuring oxalate in urine was flawed. Using a more accurate method it appears hardly any ascorbic acid is converted to oxalate in vivo. This removes every vestige of the original suggestion that ascorbic acid would increase the risk of oxalate kidney stones. Even this is not necessary, since no cases of oxalate kidney stones caused by ascorbic acid have been reported. Any physicians who can now continue to believe ascorbic acid causes kidney stones will believe they can fly by flapping their ears.

I am not clear how a vitamin dependency differs from a vitamin deficiency.

It took a long time to establish the reality of vitamin deficiencies. Folk medicine practitioners had known for many centuries that certain foods such as citrus fruits would prevent and cure scurvy. Sir James Cook sailed the seas without the usual epidemics of scurvy among his crews as he ensured they ate Vitamin C rich foods. Sir James Lind completed the first published controlled experiment proving this. Two sailors out of eight were given citrus fruits and were well in a few days. The remainder did not respond to the specifics of that day such as inhaling Earth's vapors. These were the tranquilizers of the orthodoxy of 1750. The British navy waited for forty years and the deaths of 100,000 sailors from scurvy before acting and issuing lime rations to their men. The navy physicians in the Admirality did not like Dr. Lind. Had the navy not been issued limes, sixty years later Napoleon might have invaded Great Britain successfully. But by then British sailors could stay at sea for long periods without scurvy while French sailors had to remain close to shore to prevent scurvy. The American navy ignored the British experiences with scurvy for another century.

The vitamin concept received another setback when that preeminent pathologist, Rudolf Virchow, declared no disease could be caused by a deficiency of anything. That was during the heyday of bacterial discoveries. The work on beri-beri and polished rice kept alive the idea essential factors were present in bran and germ. Much earlier, Frapolli in Italy had suggested corn caused pellagra. In 1906 Casimir Funk coined the word "vitamine" from his idea these factors were amines and vital to the body. Later, when it was clear that they were not all amines, the word was shortened to "vitamin." Funk's decision to create a name for these accessory or essential factors was a stroke of genius, for nothing really exists in human minds unless it has a name. Now one could think about vitamins.

Dr. Elmer McCollum showed that a fat-soluble factor prevented a disease of the eye called xerophthalmia. He thought it was the first of a number of factors and called it vitamin A. His views were not very popular among the medical fraternity because bacteria were still considered the cause of most diseases. This idea was so powerful that even after he had proven pellagra was caused by a junk diet too rich in corn, Goldberger felt he had to inject himself with scrapings from pellagrins to prove it was not due to an infection. It was not. McCollum made himself even more unpopular because he began to talk about his discovery to the public in lectures and the lay press.

By 1935, vitamins were accepted by physicians as essential factors, but unfortunately they were turned over to professors of biochemistry. There were few nutritional physicians teaching clinical nutrition. Professors of biochemistry then, as now, introduced medical students to vitamins in such a way as effectively to kill interest in them. In contrast to drugs, which have a special division of medicine called pharmacology devoted to them, vitamins are taught as a series of molecules which have certain chemical and physiological properties. Every doctor knows we need antibiotics for infections. Every doctor knows we all get enough vitamins from our food. It is a problem for dieticians and nutritionists, not healers. Dieticians and nutritionists happily took on the burden of dealing with vitamins in isolation from disease. They believe their own propaganda that a "balanced diet" (undefined), will provide everyone with sufficient vitamins.

Professors of biochemistry remained unaware of the discoveries by many physicians that some patients needed large amounts of vitamins. These professors tend to read biochemical journals, not medical journals. As it became clearer vitamins were often needed in large amounts, a new concept arose. Until then, only deficiency states were recognized: if one eats a diet too low in thiamine, one gets beri-beri; if the diet is too low in vitamin C, scurvy; if too low in vitamin D, rickets. A deficiency occurs when the problem is in the diet. That person's requirements are normal.

However, there are people whose requirements are so high that no diet can provide enough of certain vitamins. One can calculate the average consumption of any vitamin by analyzing one's food. One can assume this amount will, on the average, maintain the group's health. But an average is a statistical artifact which has little application to any individual. Among any large group, the amount needed will cluster about the average, but many will need much more or much less. Biological variation is well established for almost any measurable variable. Roger Williams and his colleagues have been most influential in establishing the essential variability of nutritional requirements. The almost universal variability curve is bell-shaped. But one must be careful to define what state of health is desired. If one is content to be just healthy enough to avoid dying from scurvy or rickets, one will draw one curve. If one hopes for optimum health (long, healthy life), one will draw another curve. The average amount of nutrient needed for the second distribution curve will be much higher. This is shown in the figure below.

FIGURE 1. *Optimum requirement for thiamine*

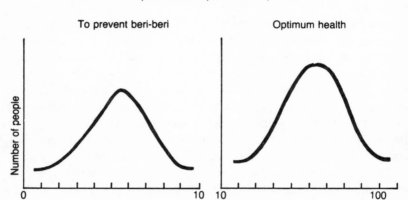

Obviously, anyone who values his/her health will want to have optimum health rather than to be just this side of scurvy, beri-beri or pellagra.

A person whose requirements are on the high side is then said to be dependent. The need for that nutrient is so great that no diet could provide enough.

A vitamin dependency can be present from birth or may be acquired. It may be so severe that infants are seriously affected and will die unless given large doses of that nutrient each day from infancy. Or a dependency may develop later on in life. A person may have a marginal adequacy of any nutrient. Under any stress such as severe infection, starvation, surgery, or even a stay in most modern hospitals, the demand for the nutrient increases and may precipitate a dependency.

Can a person develop a vitamin dependency?

Yes. The following factors create dependency:

LONG-TERM VITAMIN DEFICIENCY

Fifty years ago it was found that chronic pellagrans required more vitamin B3 than did pellagrans who had been ill only a short time; up to 600 mg per day were needed. Dogs given black tongue, canine pellagra, for many months did not recover until they were given large amounts of vitamin B3.

The classic experiment conducted by the Germans and Japanese during the last war also demonstrated the creation of a dependency by deprivation. In the Far East, allied prisoners of war were incarcerated in horribly monstrous camps for up to forty-four months. The death rate for these camps was around 25 percent or more. The German concentration camps were even worse. Most of the ex-POWs, at least those in Canada, have remained ill from the time of their incarceration on. A Canadian government survey of ex-POWs from the Far East compared them with ex-POWs from Germany. Brothers were matched. The ex-POWs of the Japanese were much sicker. There was a very high incidence of degenerative physical and psychiatric disorders.

I have treated perhaps a dozen of these ex-POWs with niacin, up to 3 grams per day. They recovered within a few weeks. One of my patients had been ill from his discharge in 1944 to 1960. During that time he had accumulated a file with the Department of Veterans' Affairs that required a large cardboard box to hold it all. Because of his persistent complaints of arthritis, severe pain, insomnia, heat and cold intolerance and nervousness, he was sent to a veterans' hospital for psychiatric evaluation. This added another burden, a psychiatric label. After that he required psychotherapy from a warm, sympathetic psychiatrist which restored him to his previous chronically sick state but freed him of the psychiatric burden. In 1960 he started to take niacin, 1 gram three times per day. Within two weeks he was well. Two years later he forgot to take his niacin with him when he went to the mountains and by the time he arrived home his symptoms had begun to come back. He never forgot to take his niacin again. He had a niacin dependency caused by 44 months of severe malnutrition and, of course, stress.

SEVERE STRESS

I have seen a large number of patients who dated the onset of their illness from the time they had been treated in hospital, usually for surgery. From observing what happens in hospital I can reconstruct the following scenarios: The patients have just been getting by with a marginal adjustment to their food. In hospital they are exposed to the stress of the surgery. For a few days they will be on intravenous fluids only, further depleting their nutrient supplies. When they are started on food it may be a soft diet. In one case I saw each meal offered after a serious hip operation. The food offered over the next six days would have depleted anyone's nutrient supplies. There was hardly an item which could be considered food. The first meal consisted of a bowl of jello, cold chicken soup, a bottle of ginger ale and a slice of white bread. The same quality of food was sustained thereafter.

In any one year in the United States about 500,000 patients suffer from malnutrition which compromises their chances for recovery. The combination of junk food, stress and a marginal state before admission precipitates a state of vitamin dependency.

A JUNK FOOD DIET

A vitamin dependency will be produced by a combination of all three factors. The more severe and prolonged the operation of each factor, the more rapidly will dependency be created. Fortunately, the most severe dependency, *e.g.*, the one suffered by ex-POWs, will respond to niacin, 3 grams per day, as well as a mild dependency will.

Do you use all the vitamins?

All of the vitamins are needed in optimum amounts. Only a few have been used in large doses, and these will be discussed. There is no doubt that in time, for every vitamin there will be a subset of the population who will require large quantities. I will deal only with those vitamins used in the treatment of schizophrenia, chiefly vitamin B3, vitamin B6, ascorbic acid and, to a lesser degree, folic acid and vitamin B12.

Vitamin B3 appears to be your favorite vitamin. Will you elaborate about its beneficial effects and possible toxicity?

This was the third B vitamin to be established as a vitamin. Both forms, niacin, known to chemists as nicotinic acid, and niacinamide, known as nicotinamide, are converted in the body to nicotinamide adenine dinucleotide (NAD). This is the anti-pellagra coenzyme. There is a continual cycle from tryptophan to niacinamide, to NAD, to niacin, to niacinamide, to NAD; the pyridine nucleotide cycle.

These forms of B3 are not identical in properties and have different indications for treatment. Niacin causes a vasodilation or flush when first taken which usually begins in the forehead and gradually advances down the rest of the body, rarely involving the whole body to the toes. The flush lasts several hours and the first reaction is the worst. In most people the flush eventually no longer occurs or is very slight. The intensity of the flush varies with the dose: with 50 mg doses hardly anyone flushes, with 1 gram doses nearly everyone does. A few patients can not tolerate the flush at all. If niacin is very important, the flush can be reduced by pretreatment for two days with aspirin or antihistamines. The niacin flush resembles that produced by histamine injections and is probably due to a massive release of histamine. Very rarely an intense flush will cause transient faintness. It is impossible to predict who will have the most intense flush. Elderly people, arthritics, schizophrenics, alcoholics and dark-skinned people tend to flush less than average. Niacinamide is the non-flushing form of B3 but, inexplicably, about 1 percent of the people who take it will have a mild flush. Niacin esters such as inositol niacinate (Linodil) and xanthene niacinate cause no flush or a very mild one. Slow-release preparations reduce the flush. Niacin normalizes blood fat and cholesterol levels: lowering cholesterol levels if too high, elevating them if too low, it elevates high-density lipoproteins and lowers low-density lipoproteins. Niacinamide has no effect on blood fats.

As I told you, the initial dose for both forms of vitamin B3 is 1 gram taken three times per day. The dose is increased if the therapeutic response is too slight or too slow. It is seldom possible to go over 6 grams per day with niacinamide; at higher doses nausea and later vomiting may develop and this must not be permitted. With niacin it is possible to go much higher. A few patients on their own have gone as high as 30 grams per day and more. Each person has a limit which must not be exceeded. If the nauseant dose is too low, both forms of B3 may be used in combination to achieve a 3 gram per day level.

When the dose has been established it is maintained until the patient is well and thereafter for a long period of time to ensure continuing health. Many will have to take it for life, for schizophrenia is a long-term biochemical dysfunction, comparable to diabetes mellitus. Many patients feel so much better on niacin that they see no point in discontinuing it. I began to use niacin myself in 1954. I was well and did not expect any beneficial effect. I took it because I wanted to test its effect on me, especially the flush, but also the long-term effect. I found the flush difficult to adjust to for a few months. Since then it has not been a problem. I have been using niacin since then, usually at a 3 gram daily dosage.

When I first began to take niacin I did have a problem with bleeding gums. Neither ascorbic acid nor my dentist nor cleaning my teeth helped. I concluded that there was nothing I could do and accepted it. To my surprise, after two weeks on niacin my gums were firm and no longer bled. This observation led to our discovery that niacin lowered cholesterol levels. Later I noticed a second change: I had more energy and required less sleep. I gained about three useful hours each day.

The only side effect I have noted occurred a couple of years ago when I developed slight edema of my ankles. This vanished when I lowered my dose to 2 grams per day for a few months. For the past year I have been taking 3 grams per day. I have been on a niacin for thirty years and have consumed just under 30 kg (66 pounds). I remain well.

In addition to treating schizophrenia, vitamin B3 is used to treat some children with learning and behavioral disorders, addicts, alcoholics, and as an adjunct to diet for hypoglycemics. It is very helpful for treating arthritis, senility, and a few other confusional states. It is an antidote to lysergic acid diethylamide (LSD). Post-electroconvulsive memory loss and confusion are reduced by niacin. Its normalizing action on blood fats and lipids is used for treating high cholesterol levels and cardiovascular disease. It forms, combined with Colestipol, the only effective treatment for familial hypercholesterolemia. At last these unfortunate patients have a chance for a normal lifespan.

One should know the side effects. They are not toxic, but can be unpleasant if not dealt with. Before anyone uses any therapeutic compound, they should be aware of possible negative effects. This applies to every compound. Medical reference books describing drugs for physicians list the indications and also toxicity and side effects. Every known negative effect is listed, but they never report how frequent that complication is. A side effect which appears in 25 percent of the people is listed in the same way as one which appears in one out of 10,000 cases. As a result, an enormous number of effects are listed. Physicians understand this and will not be deterred by toxicity which occurs rarely when the result of treatment is beneficial. Treatment is monitored so that incipient side effects are detected. The advantage in listing every side effect without a probability value for its occurrence is that it protects drug companies and alerts physicians, but it also neutralizes the toxic side effect impact. If tardive dyskinesia is listed as a tranquilizer side effect equally prominently with skin discoloration which is very rare, one becomes less concerned over the very important neurological side effect. There are other disadvantages: many patients consult these books before filling the prescription and become terrified when they read the entire list of side effects.

Vitamin B3 is described in the same physicians' drug reference books in a few paragraphs. There will be perhaps two lines of indications and a few lines of negative effects. In sharp contrast, every drug used in treating schizophrenia has several pages of material, most of it dealing with side effects. A quick way of judging the relative safety of a compound is to divide the number of lines used to list indications by the number of lines used to describe its adverse effects. A high number measures safety and a low number shows the degree of toxicity. For example here are a few indices of safety for a number of vitamins and other therapeutic compounds used in treating schizophrenia.

| Product | Number of Lines Describing | | Ratio |
	A) Indications	B) Adverse Effects	$\frac{A}{B} \times 10$
Vitamin E	6	2	30
Vitamin B6	13	3	43
Vitamin C	7	7	24
Linodil	3	2	15
Niacin	3	2	6
Chlorpromazine	6	87	0.7
Stelazine	6	94	0.6
Haldol	2	81	0.2
Elavil	3	46	0.6
Tofranil	12	42	2.8
Valium	13	23	5.6

From: Compendium Pharmaceuticals
and Specialties, 19th Ed., 1984

Drugs are owned by companies; they are patented. These companies have medical personnel who ensure that toxicity or negative side effects are not exaggerated. On the other hand, no one really cares what is written about vitamins and the descriptions contain gross inaccuracies. The compilers of the Canadian *Compendium of Pharmaceuticals and Specialties*, 1984, in describing niacin would write something to the effect that it is *alleged* to lower cholesterol levels. This was written after several thousand scientific papers all reporting the same thing, and long after the Food and Drug Administration sanctioned it officially for this use—and the FDA has never been noted for its friendliness toward vitamins. Many years ago I wrote to the Canadian editor, bringing this error to his attention. It took over three years before they improved the wording slightly. Yet the description of a drug used to lower cholesterol, now banned in several countries in Europe, was scrutinized in detail by the medical officers of the company owning the patents. Of course, these compendiums are financed by drug companies. Listing vitamins does not get them much support.

Vitamin B3 has the following side effects:

1. Flushing in 100 percent by niacin, in less than one percent by niacinamide.

2. Nausea and later vomiting. This is dose-related. When the dose goes high enough, it will occur in almost everyone. With niacinamide over 6 grams daily will cause this in up to 50 percent. With niacin one can go much higher. Using 3 grams daily nausea and vomiting may occur in under 2 percent. Usually if one form can not be used, one can safely use the other. One in 500 patients may be sensitive to even 100 mg doses.

3. Liver disease. About one in 2000 developing jaundice of an obstructive type. It clears within a few weeks when the vitamin is stopped. In a few patients, resuming the niacin did not bring back the jaundice. No deaths have been reported.

Physicians have been disturbed by abnormal liver function tests. About 30 years ago, studies by the Mayo Clinic showed that patients showing these abnormalities had normal livers when liver was examined by microscope. They could see no evidence of liver damage. They concluded the elevated test results were an in vitro artifact, the result of niacin interfering with the test.

The question of liver damage arose in 1950 when it was reported that niacin in large doses caused fatty livers in rats. This fitted the belief then fashionable that methyl group deficiency was a cause of liver damage. Niacin binds methyl groups. It was then reasonable to assume too much niacin would take out too much of the methyl radicals and cause a methyl deficiency disease. However, many years later, Prof. R. Altschul, Chairman, Department of Anatomy, University of Saskatchewan, repeated these rat experiments using the same large doses of niacin. These rats did not develop fatty livers and examination of their livers by electron microscope revealed no pathological changes. Further, when niacin does cause jaundice, it is the obstructive type which clears rapidly.

Fatty livers heal very slowly and are much more dangerous than obstructive jaundice.

Vitamin B3 was given an undeserved bad name by research which could not be corroborated later on using more advanced technology.

4. Darkening of the skin. This is a harmless darkening of the skin, usually in the flexor areas of the body, which occurs very rarely, in perhaps 1 out of 2000 cases.

    I have seen only one case in the last ten years. It is due to the deposition of melanin, occurs almost entirely in schizophrenics and clears in a year or so. It is easily removed by gently rubbing the area after a bath when it will leave clear, normally-pigmented skin. It is the body's way of getting rid of the schizophrenic chrome indole melanin pigments (rheo melanin). I have seen the same colored pigment deposited in nails which eventually grow out clear as the patient recovers. It is *not* nigricans.

5. Very rarely it causes slight edema of the ankles, especially in warm weather. When this happens the dose must be reduced and one form of B3 may have to be replaced by another.

6. Even more rare is a difficulty with vision, with was reported in only two cases over fifteen years ago. There have been no reports since then. Vision cleared promptly when the niacin was stopped.

7. There are a few minor biochemical changes such as elevation of uric acid. It does not aggravate gout. (Neither does it treat gout.)

One of the reasons psychiatrists cannot believe that vitamin B3 helps schizophrenics is their failure to understand how a vitamin could have an effect on the brain, even for those who at least recognize that there is a brain dysfunction in schizophrenia. When we first published our clinical results in 1957, we listed a number of ways this can happen. Recent research into the relationship between neurohormones and brain receptors has revealed two more possible ways. Several years ago it was found that niacinamide acted on the same neuron receptor as Valium. It also shares properties with Valium but has none of Valium's negative properties. This work showed vitamin B3 to be natural substance which bound to these receptors.

Not surprisingly, more recent work establishes NAD as a neurohormone involved with another one, gamma-amino-butyric acid (GABA). NAD is a calming neurohormone.

Dr. Hoffer, I just read in the Medical Tribune, April 24, 1985, that niacin decreases mortality and increases longevity.

That is correct. What I found surprising was the surprise of the headline writer. After my colleagues and I had demonstrated niacin lowered cholesterol levels, Dr. Ed Boyle treated about 160 patients after one coronary for ten years. On the niacin only six died instead of the expected 60.

The huge Coronary Drug Project conducted between 1966 and 1975 in over 50 hospitals on nearly 8500 men was recently updated. Dr. P. L. Canner ("Mortality in Coronary Drug Project patients during a nine-year post-treatment period," *Journal of the American College of Cardiology*, vol. 5, page 422, 1985) in a recent report claimed that niacin decreased mortality 11 percent and increased longevity two years compared to every other treatment studied. As a result, the National Institutes of Health now recommend to every physician for patients with elevated cholesterol levels that they try to bring them down by proper nutrition, and use niacin to lower them if diet fails. In other words, NIH is now promoting megavitamin (B3) therapy.

You also have me taking large doses of vitamin C. Why? Is it safe?

Ascorbic acid, vitamin C, is needed in much larger quantities than other vitamins. Even the RDAs recognize this, placing its daily requirement around 50 mg per day. None of the other vitamins comes even close to this recommended amount. I. Stone did not accept ascorbic acid as a vitamin. To him it was a major metabolite, more like an amino acid. Since no one can make any in the body, everyone suffers from a genetic disease called hypoascorbemia.

During evolution, man and other primates lost the ability to convert glucose to ascorbic acid. This provided an evolutionary advantage for our ancestors; living on a diet rich enough in ascorbic acid, they needed no further endogenous supplies. Linus Pauling (1968) provided an explanation for this apparent paradox. How could there be any advantage in becoming dependent upon food for all the ascorbic acid needed? Pauling showed that the energy gained by the cells in not having to make ascorbic acid allowed other processes to develop which provided the advantage. But any advantage disappears as soon as the diet becomes deficient in the vitamin. This happened when we moved from a diet very rich in ascorbic acid to one containing very small amounts; gorillas in their native habitate consume several grams of ascorbic acid per day. These evolutionary changes are irreversible. Once we lost our biochemical system for making ascorbic acid there was no turning back; we will remain dependent on external sources forever.

The optimum amount of ascorbic acid varies from person to person and time to time. Irwin Stone showed that the greater the stress, the greater the threat to life, the more ascorbic acid was required. Dr. Robert Cathcart found that one could find this optimum by using a titration procedure: the daily dose is increased until gas and diarrhea develop and are present for more than a few days. This is the diarrhea or laxative dose, and for people who are constipated it may be the best dose. For others the sublaxative dose is used, a few grams below the laxative dose. This dose varies enormously, usually from 1 to 40 grams per day when ascorbic acid it dissolved in liquid. When the dry powder is swallowed much more may be taken. One woman suffering from severe withdrawal reaction from suddenly stopping tranquilizers took 250 grams per day for five days with no laxative effect.

Higher doses can be given intravenously using ascorbates, mineral salts of ascorbic acid. Commonly, 60 grams are added to 1 liter of IV fluid; one can inject up to two liters per day if needed. Giving it intravenously provides a uniform high concentration of ascorbic acid. A single oral dose allows a rapid build-up in the blood and a rapid decline. One could approximate IV use by giving oral doses every 30 minutes, every hour, and so on. I treated my first schizophrenic patient with high doses of ascorbic acid in 1952, giving her 1 gram per hour, day and night. Her psychosis cleared in three days and her

skin, ulcerated over cancer of the breast following surgery and radiation, began to heal.

Below are some guidelines in determining how much ascorbic
acid to advise patients to start with.

Grams/day	Indications
1–3	To maintain health
3–10	Infections: virus, colds
	Allergies
	All diseases
10–100	Cancer
	Severe infections: viral, bacterial
	Snake and insect bites
	Intoxications

After the patient is well, the dose is reduced to a maintenance
level which again varies with the individual.

Ascorbic acid is extraordinarily safe. Nevertheless, a vitamin C
toxicity mythology has been created among the medical profession
based upon sloppy research and extravagant projections from possibility to fact. The most serious allegation was that ascorbic acid would
cause formation of kidney stones. This was based upon a finding
made many years ago that some ascorbic acid was metabolized to
oxalate in the body. Recently, a review of this work showed this was
wrong. The method originally used was wrong. The oxalate was
created in the test tube from the ascorbic acid in the urine; it did not
happen in the body. After the original report it was suggested that
ascorbic acid *might* be hazardous to habitual oxalate kidney stone
formers. Before long, Victor Herbert was on a North American
lecture tour advising doctors that vitamin C could cause kidney
stones. This is also what they teach about ascorbic acid at Loma
Linda Medical School and probably at every other medical school
as well. What Victor Herbert does not tell anyone is that so far no
cases have have been reported, that kidney specialists ignore this idea
and that there is no basis in theory or in fact for this belief. Yet,
patients are unnecessarily frightened by well-meaning but ignorant
nutritionists and physicians.

A deficiency of pyridoxine is much more likely to cause oxalate kidney stones. E. J. Will and L. M. Bijvoet (*Metabolism*, 28:542-548, 1979) reported that 1 gram per day decreased oxalate excretion in two patients with primary oxalosis by 65 percent.

Victor Herbert alone is responsible for establishing a second myth, that ascorbic acid destroys vitamin B12 and may therefore cause pernicious anemia. He added ascorbic acid to a test meal containing B12. Using a method useful for blood but not for food, he reported a loss of vitamin B12. However, a method known to be accurate for food vitamin B12 showed no loss whatever. Nor have any cases of pernicious anemia arising out of ascorbic acid therapy been reported.

There are two possible side effects from ascorbic acid: The laxative effect has been described; the other is the development of allergic reactions either to the tablet fillers or to the ascorbic acid itself. A few patients have reacted to as little as 50 mg. Obviously, this is a reaction to traces of impurities in the synthetic ascorbic acid. It resembles allergic reactions to every kind of pill or drug or vitamin available.

Ascorbic acid usually works slowly except when it is used to treat scurvy. I expect little response until several weeks have passed. A few very sick schizophrenics respond rapidly. One of my patients did not respond to heavy doses of tranquilizers. She remained very tense and agitated and paced the corridors of the University Hospital relentlessly, wearing out her shoes and the soles of her feet. Three days after starting on 10 grams per day she was freed of her agitation.

People who use ascorbic acid to maintain good health can judge its effect by a general sense of well-being and fewer colds.

Ascorbic acid acts on the receptor area in the brain responsive to the tranquilizer haloperidol (Haldol). Since ascorbic acid is a natural substance in the brain, and Haldol is not, it is more appropriate to consider that these are ascorbic acid receptors on neurones and that Haldol binds to the same centers. Ascorbic acid is water-soluble and crosses the blood/brain barrier with difficulty. Only one-half of one percent of the oral dose gets across. Haldol crosses much more readily. We need ascorbic acid attached to a substance which will transport it across this barrier. This would make ascorbic acid an excellent, safe anti-anxiety or anti-tension substance. A combination of Haldol and ascorbic acid, if this were possible, could be a very potent, safe tranquilizer.

Didn't you mention that you also use pyridoxine for some patients?

Pyridoxine, vitamin B6, is used in a dose range under 2000 mg per day. Most patients need less than 500 mg per day. It may be used orally, intravenously or intramuscularly. At these doses it is safe. At doses of 2000 mg per day and much higher a few patients have developed neurological complications which cleared when the pyridoxine was discontinued. But it is not clear whether other factors were involved, since the report gave no information about the nutritional state of the six cases. The authors of the report were so delighted to find these cases that they immediately began to demand the sale of pyridoxine be controlled, labeling it a neurotoxin. The authors had to scout several medical schools to locate these cases. This is an indication how safe it is. I have never seen any side effects, nor have any orthomolecular therapists reported any. In children one must ensure they have enough magnesium; a few have become irritable on pyridoxine but this does not happen when they are given magnesium.

Recently, Dr. Mary Coleman has found that the neurological changes seen after very large doses of pyridoxine are due to a deficiency of vitamin B3. This may be why orthomolecular physicians see none; they use B3 in association with B6.

Pyridoxine is most often given with zinc, especially for patients with too much kryptopyrrole (KP), which can be measured by a simple urine test. KP binds both pyridoxine and zinc, causing a double deficiency. Patients excreting KP were called Malvarians before it was identified. They are now termed *pyroluriacs*. This is one of the schizophrenic syndromes described by Carl Pfeiffer and his associates.

About one-third of schizophrenic patients have pyroluria. They are typically schizophrenic but have more insight and their mood is more appropriate. These schizophrenics also have white spots on their nails, loss of dreaming or cannot recall dreams, sweetish breath odor, stretch marks, inability to tan and sensitivity to sunlight. They may also be impotent, have menstrual irregularities and anemia unresponsive to iron. They need up to 1 gram per day of B6, and zinc, and respond well.

You also have me taking some zinc. Can you explain why?

Zinc is an essential water-soluble mineral. On the average, healthy people need about 15 mg per day. Many eat much less, especially patients in institutions. Because zinc salts are water-soluble, they are leached out of soils, especially sandy soils. Soils cropped for many years lose zinc to the crops which are removed. Some soils found in Egypt, Iran and Iraq contain almost no zinc.

Severe zinc deficiency prevents growth and sexual development. These severe symptoms are very rare in people living in other areas. However, zinc deficiency less severe leads to a large number of symptoms: skin may show stretch marks, hair and nails do not grow well, nails may have white spots, and a severe form of acne may appear on the face. Sexual development may be delayed. Menses may appear late. Young males may be impotent. There may be joint pain, retarded wound healing and loss of taste.

Zinc deficiency may cause one of the schizophrenic syndromes.

A number of zinc preparations are available, providing a choice. Some find one type may cause nausea due to the zinc salt being used and may find another form easier to tolerate. Zinc sulfate 220 mg is equivalent to 60 mg of zinc. Zinc gluconate is also available, as are various zinc chelates. I seldom advise more than 50 mg of zinc per day.

I have found a large proportion of elderly patients I have seen, especially when there is a memory problem, have high blood copper and low zinc levels, with a very high copper-over-zinc ratio. Adding zinc may reduce copper levels and increase zinc levels.

Carl Pfeiffer's and his colleagues' books should be consulted. They are the best source of accurate clinical information relating zinc metabolism to schizophrenia and other psychiatric illnesses.

You assured me I would not get tardive dyskinesia when I had to use tranquilizers. How can you be so sure?

Because I am seeing that you get manganese. A person loses 4 mg per day of this water-soluble mineral, which plays a role in the treatment of schizophrenia. Combined with zinc, it helps lower elevated copper levels.

Tranquilizers may bind with manganese to cause a deficiency. According to Dr. R. Kunin, this is the cause of tardive dyskinesia, which can be prevented by giving small amounts of manganese and treated effectively by this mineral. A few patients do not respond until niacin is also added. Dr. David Hawkins reported that he had seen no cases of tardive dyskinesia in over 10,000 schizophrenic patients treated over twenty years. This has been my experience as well. Tardive dyskinesia is such a serious toxic reaction that it must not be permitted to occur. The information about manganese and tardive dyskinesia has been available long enough that no psychiatrist can be excused for having permitted patients to develop it. It may take a few lawsuits for negligence before institutions and their psychiatric staff take this seriously.

Drug companies may one day add enough manganese to each tranquilizer tablet to remove tardive dyskinesis as one of the side effects.

I have heard that Dr. D. O. Rudin has an exciting new book coming out which describes the importance of Omega-3 essential fatty acids in nutrition. Could you give me a very few highlights?

Dr. Rudin, in a book soon to be published, *The Omega Factor and the Lifestyle Diseases*, describes how a deficiency of Omega-3 essential fatty acids is responsible for a major portion of the dominant diseases of modernized societies such as heart, bowel and immune diseases, psychoses, delinquency, cancer, arthritis, dandruff, dry skin, obesity and tooth decay. These resemble the chronic B-vitamin deficiency diseases of beri-beri and pellagra, lipid deficiency diseases, lipid oxidation diseases, lipid-like endocrine diseases and premature aging which have developed chiefly in the past hundred years.

Rudin lists eight essential nutrient factors:

1. Water
2. Minerals
3. Proteins (amino acids)
5. Lipids (essential fatty acids)
6. Carbohydrates (dietary fiber)
7. Bacteria
8. Calories

Only one of the above has not been associated with the characteristic deficiency diseases, because the symptoms are vague, diffuse and widespread. This is due to the presence of two families of essential fatty acids, the omega-6 and the omega-3. The omega-3 are the cold-climate essential fatty acids and are important constituents of nervous tissue. These unsaturated fatty acids have lower freezing points; animals and plants need this protection against freezing. Cold adaptation is merely an increase in the amount of these essential fatty acids in the tissues.

The omega-3 essential fatty acids have been removed from our food by a number of processes peculiar to modern industrialized society, the process of converting food to more expensive junk:

1. Chemical treatment, including hydrogenation of fats, fertilization, acid rain and chlorination and fluoridation of water.
2. Mechanical effects which remove germ and husk.
3. Transportation, which moves warm-country oils to areas which require cold-adapted oils, and introduces exotic foods into the general diet.
4. Hyperagriculturalization, including heavy cropping, fertilization and acid rain as well as increasing replacement of indigenous foods by exotic foods.
5. Administrative effects, short-sighted decisions by government agencies which decrease the amount of omega-3 essential fatty acids in food.

The omega-6 essential fatty acids have the first double-bond six carbons from the methyl end, as follows:

Alpha-linoleic acid	2 double bonds
Gamma-linolenic acid	3 double bonds
Arachidonic acid	4 double bonds

The omega-3 series have the first double bond three carbons from the methyl end. It includes:

Alpha-linolenic acid	3 double bonds
Linoleneic acid	4 double bonds
Eicosapentaenoic acid (EPA)	5 double bonds
Docosapentaenoic acid	6 double bonds

The two families of essential fatty acids are not interconvertible, but they do influence each other's metabolism, as the same enzymes work on both. These fatty acids are converted into prostaglandins. The omega-3 fats are converted into prostaglandins series 1 and 2, and the omega-6 into prostaglandin series 3 (PG3). These prostaglandins are involved in an enormous number of biochemical and physiological reactions. When there is a deficiency in essential fatty acids these reactions break down or are distorted, leading to a large number of signs and symptoms. This may cause disease in eye, ear, joints, in the immune regulatory defense system, in nearly every transaction in the brain, in skin lesions, in endocrine disorders, cardiovascular pathology and in defects in cold adaptation.

Most of the nutrients are involved in the formation and metabolism of the prostaglandins. A deficiency of prostaglandins of one type will cause an imbalance in the ratios of the prostaglandin series. This, according to to Rudin, is one of the main causes of a large number of modern degeneraive diseases. A deficiency will arise from a deficiency in substrate, i.e., in the essential fatty acid or in a deficiency of essential nutrients, such as the B vitamins which are necessary to convert essential fatty acids to prostaglandins. If there are adequate supplies of essential fatty acids but a deficiency of B vitamins, disease develops due to a lack of prostaglandins. Giving more essential fatty acids will have only a slight effect. If there is a deficiency of omega-3 essential fatty acids, giving more vitamins will have only a slight effect since there is too little substrate present. This explains why some respond well to vitamins while others do not. Ideally, there must be an optimum amount of both substrate and vitamins to yield the optimum quantity of the three prostaglandin series, PG1, PG2, and PG3.

The best sources of Omega-3 essential fatty acids are foods indigenous to cold climates; plants growing in northern U.S.A. and Canada, cold-adapted animals and fish found in cold waters are the best sources. People living in warm areas where cold adaptation is not a problem will not need as much. The need is also determined by one's heritage. West Coast Indians in Canada traditionally eat large amounts of salmon, a cold-water fish. On this diet they remain well. Celtic people traditionally eat large quantities of fish and presumably develop a need for omega-3 essential fatty acids. When they are deprived of these fats they become ill. It has been suggested the Irish are more susceptible to alcoholism because they are deficient in omega-3 essential fatty acids. Giving some evening primrose oil has removed the desire for alcohol.

The best practical sources are shown in the following table.

Source	Problems	Amount Required*
Linseed oil	Becomes rancid easily and develops bad taste	1 to 6 tablespoons per day
Evening primrose oil	Very expensive	1 to 6 capsules per day
Cod liver oil	Bad taste	1 to 6 capsules per day
Canola oil	——	As used in normal cooking
Fish oils	——	1 to 6 capsules per day
Cold-adapted foods	May be hard to get	Normal diet

*These are estimates. Each person must work out his optimum amount by observing how he feels.

Lipid tests for blood are being developed which may help us determine who requires which essential fatty acid, but these laboratories are not generally available.

A practical therapeutic test is required. It is not dangerous, since essential fatty acids are nutrients. Any person following the nutrition rules already described *should* be well, but, many wil not be because they have requirements for nutrients above those available even on a good diet. They should then examine their diet to see if there are deficiencies there. They can then add nutrients, especially the B vitamins, vitamin C and essential fatty acids. The most efficient way is to take a wide variety of nutrients. Once they are as well as they want to be or are content with their state of health, they should hold their nutrient maintenance steady for three to six months. Later they can reduce the quantity or withdraw one nutrient at a time to determine their need. If they find they do not feel as good, they should resume the dose which kept them well.

AMINO ACIDS

I am not taking any pure amino acids as supplements. Are these not important?

In orthomolecular medicine, the 1960s marked the megavitamin decade, the 1970s the mineral decade and the 1980s will be the amino acid decade. The essential fatty acids will also share the 1980s and run into the 1990s. By "amino acid decade" I mean the decade in which individual amino acids will be used as supplements for a number of diseases or problems. Until now, nutritionists were concerned only in ensuring that the essential amino acids were provided as a group. Free amino acids were used primarily for intravenous nutrition and patients unable to digest protein; the latter group took them orally.

In the genetic disease phenylketonuria (PKU), phenylalanine cannot be metabolized properly. This condition affects babies, who grow up mentally retarded unless given a special diet very low in phenylalanine. Since tyrosine is made from phenylalanine, there may be a deficiency of tyrosine.

Tryptophan has been studied more intensively than any other single amino acid. In the body it is a substrate for a number of substances including vitamin B3 (about 1.5 percent is converted) and serotonin. Tryptophan is used to help some patients achieve sleep and helps up to half of them. It must be taken on an empty stomach so that it will be able to enter the brain without having to compete with other amino acids. It also has some antidepressant properties, especially when combined with vitamin B3. Perhaps the vitamin forces more of the amino acid to be changed into serotonin. Many years ago it was used to accelerate healing of the skin of pellagrins.

L-tryptophan is safe, but is very expensive and available primarily in health food stores.

Histidine is converted into histamine in the body and is therefore a very important amino acid. Histamine is a neurohormone. Carl Pfeiffer has described its role in subtypes of schizophrenia: some have too little histamine (histapenia), and others have too much (histadelia).

Tyrosine is a precursor of noradrenalin and adrenalin and may play a role in treating conditions characteristic of noradrenalin deficiency. It has been used to treat depression.

The ratio of leucine to isoleucine is related to pellagra. An excess of leucine increases the loss of vitamin B3 into the urine. This is reversed by isoleucine. Most foods have more leucine than isoleucine, except for watermelon, which has more isoleucine. Watermelon might be a good antidote to corn, which has too much leucine and too little isoleucine. In a few cases I have found isoleucine, 3 grams per day, helpful for acute schizophrenia.

Cysteine, cystine, taurine and methionine are sulfer-containing amino acids. The first three are made in the body from methionine. Carl Pfeiffer described the use of methionine with other nutrients for histadelic schizophrenics.

This is a sketchy outline of amino acids. We must have controlled studies for each amino acid to determine indications, how much to use and with what other nutrients.

DRUGS

With all those nutrients doing all that, it hardly seems as if there'd be any need for drugs as well. But you say that you do use them in conjunction with the nutritional therapy.

In conjunction, yes. They're invaluable in getting the patient to a state in which the overall treatment can progress, preferably with his cooperation. The main problems with drugs have come from over-reliance on them and misunderstanding of what they can be expected to accomplish.

Tranquilizers and antidepressants are offshoots of the discoveries of antihistamines. A famous French surgeon, Dr. H. Laborit, first discovered the sedative-like properties of these unique antihistamines. They differ from the usual antihistamines like Benadryl by having much more central activity. From France these drugs moved to Canada and soon after to the U.S.A. They quickly swept into modern psychiatry because they are very potent and effective and much safer than any other sedative drugs like barbiturates. In contrast to vitamins, these drugs were patented. The drug companies, once they had their patents, quickly promoted their use. Within a matter of months their presence was known to all.

Treatment results were very dramatic. Patients who had been very disturbed or aggressive for years were, within a matter of days, relaxed and at ease, and no longer showed psychotic behavior. It was easy to overestimate the therapeutic effect and confuse tranquility with cure.

The general atmosphere in chronic mental hospitals changed dramatically. Psychiatrists were so surprised at the effect of tranquilizers that they could not believe what they saw and searched for "objective" evidence. One hospital recorded the effect on a whole ward by recording the general noise level of the ward, comparing the decibels of noise before and after tranquilizers were introduced. There was a dramatic decline in the noise level within a few days.

As a result of the introduction of tranquilizers, psychiatry changed drastically. Community psychiatry became possible, i.e., it became possible to discharge many chronic patients to the community. As the community made an inadequate effort to find alternate places or mini-hospitals, these patients naturally drifted to the streets. There was so much enthusiasm for this "progressive" move that few voices spoke for the patient. A more positive effect was that it accelerated development of interest in biological psychiatry and helped defeat the psychoanalytic movement which had just succeeded in taking over the philosophical center of U.S. psychiatry.

A negative effect was that it prevented any serious attention being given to vitamin therapy. The first major niacin paper showing how it helped schizophrenia appeared in 1957. No one was interested as they were all blinded by their vision of the cure of schizophrenia by tranquilizers. Tranquilizers have been a mixed blessing for patients and society.

Most schizophrenics who respond to tranquilizers have to take them for a long time, probably forever. I will here list the tranquilizers and refer to their major side effects.

Phenothiazines. The common ones are chlorpromazine (Thorazine, Largactil), thioridazine (Mellaril), fluphenazine decanoate (Modecate), fluphenazine enanthate (Moditen Enanthate), fluphenazine (Moditen), methotrimeporazene (Nozinan), trifluoperazine (Stelazine) and perphenazine (Trilafon).

Thioxanthenes. Flupenthexol (Fluanxol).

Butyrophenones. Haloperidol (Haldol).

Diphenylbutyl Piperidines. Fluspiriline (Imap) and pimozide (Orap).

Tranquilizers are taken orally or by injection. Long-acting injectable tranquilizers are released slowly from muscle where they were injected and have certain advantages: the drug is released slowly, providing steady effect, in a few are more effective than oral drugs, and they ensure that the patient is under control. Patients often dislike the side effects so much that they will not continue to take the medication. This may make the difference between living in the community or in hospital. One patient is now in hospital for the nineteenth time; each time she does not show up for her injection this is followed in a few weeks by bizarre behavior. As long as she remains on medication she is able to function and live alone in her own apartment.

Tranquilizers have a number of very serious side effects and a large number of rare side effects which are life-threatening. Nevertheless they are very safe. The major side effect is the tranquilizer syndrome. This is the reason patients so often discontinue medication; as I have outlined, they create a permanent state of dependency and make recovery impossible. This ubiquitous side effect is never described in textbooks of pharmacology, pharmacopea or package inserts.

The second major one is tardive dyskinesia. Patients develop involuntary muscle movements which affect the limbs and facial muscles. There may be a fine or coarse tremor, and sometimes there are violent movements and contortions. In many cases it is irreversible, but some patients gradually recover when the drug is withheld. However, they then run the major of risk of relapsing back into their psychosis.

Dr. R. Kunin showed that tardive dyskinesia was due to a deficiency of manganese, and that replacing the manganese quickly removed the tardive dyskinesia. His patients were also on niacin. Dr. Kunin's observations have been confirmed. His work suggests that placing the appropriate number of molecules of manganese in each tablet would prevent tardive dyskinesia from appearing. The first drug company that does so will have an immense advantage over all other drug companies, but so far none has shown any interest.

A third side effect is weight gain; many patients become obese. Part of the reason is the apathy and inertia: they burn fewer calories. However, there is also an increased desire to eat. Perhaps eating activity replaces to some degree other muscular activity which is suppressed by the drug, or perhaps tranquilizers remove self-control and judgment. No matter what the reason, I have seen this too often to ignore it. Obesity is one of the side effects which then becomes a problem to be dealt with. One of the worst problems is to try to resocialize and rehabilitate an obese, tranquilized patient.

Simply listing the remaining side effects would require several pages. Fortunately they occur very infrequently. Any unusual symptom should be reported immediately to the physician. No one should be on tranquilizers without medical supervision.

Dr. Hoffer, do you also use antidepressants?

Antidepressants are used for treating depression in both schizophrenic patients and non-schizophrenics. They may have a particular advantage for paranoid patients. About ten years ago it occurred to me that I could not recall ever having seen any patient who was both paranoid and happy at the same time. There may be some, but I have not found any during my thirty-five years of practicing psychiatry. If this was an accurate observation, would it be useful to treat paranoid patients by treating their depression with antidepressants?

I had under my care a schizophrenic man, aged about thirty, who had been sick from before puberty. He had been in some of the best private hospitals in the U.S. including a lengthy stay at the Menninger Clinic, at the Institute of Living and in a variety of other psychiatric institutions. He came under my care about twelve years ago, when he was as sick as any patient I have ever seen. I immediately began to treat him with tranquilizers (up to 800 mg of chlorpromazine per day) plus a very comprehensive nutrition and vitamin program. Within two years he was much better except that he remained very paranoid.

With my new idea in mind, I started him on clomipramine (Anafranil). Within three months his paranoid ideas were almost gone and he was much more cheerful. He has remained on this program since.

He now lives with a young family who look after his needs. He is very fond of them and they of him. Unfortunately, by the time I first got him he had already been sick for two-thirds of his life. He will never be independent, but his family has provided for his permanent care and he is freed of the major consequences of his chronic schizophrenia.

Other paranoids have responded equally well. I use the tricyclics. I do not know how monoamine oxidase inhibitors would work.

The two major types of antidepressants are monoamine oxidase (MAO) inhibitors and the tricyclics. Both have different mechanisms of action. The first group are not used as much in North America as it is believed they are more dangerous. If tricyclics do not help, psychiatrists may try MAO inhibitors. The two common ones are phenelzine sulfate (Nardil) and tranylcypromine sulfate (Parnate).

There are many more tricyclics such as clomipramine (Anafranil), amoxapine (Ascendin), amitryptiline (Elavil), desipramine (Norpramin, Pertofrane), doxepin (Sinequan), trimipramine (Surmontil) and imipramine (Tofranil). A few other types are available.

Antidepressants are relatively safe, probably safer than tranquilizers, yet they should be used only under medical supervision. They may upset many patients by increasing agitation and almost always cause a dry mouth, which is unpleasant, and may interfere with vision.

A few patients respond best to a combination of MAO inhibitors and tricyclics. This combination has an undeserved bad name based upon a few bad reactions occurring over twenty years ago. The North American package insert lists this combination as a contraindication, yet it has been used in England since both drugs were developed. I have used it for over twenty-five years. The incidence of side effects has been lower than it has been with tricyclics alone, but minimal amounts of each group are used. I usually use 20 mg of MAO inhibitor in the morning and 50 mg of tricyclic at night. Life has become normal for several patients who had never been free of depression for years or even decades.

Patients on MAO inhibitors must avoid certain foods which contain amines which are destroyed by monoamine oxidases. When these enzymes are inhibited by such drugs as Parnate or Marplan, the amines from these foods may increase in the body and elevate blood pressure. The foods which must be avoided are old ripe cheeses, red wine, liver and sardines. A few physicians also restrict other foods like bananas, but I have never seen any problems from these other foods.

I have heard you state in lectures that patients cannot be well while taking tranquilizers.

Tranquilizers are very safe compounds compared to many drugs used in medicine. This is not surprising, since they are derived from antihistamines which have been shown to be very safe. Tranquilizers are not toxic in the sense that they have a high LD-50, the amount of the drug required to kill half the animals tested. Tranquilizers do have a large number of side effects which affect a small proportion of patients, but doctors are trained to deal with side effects. The therapeutic effect is so valuable that the final outcome is less dangerous than the disease without tranquilizers. They are very effective and it would very difficult to practice psychiatry if they had not been developed.

However, there are two side effects which must be known. Tardive dyskinesia has already been described. As I have shown, it is due to a deficiency of manganese caused by the tranquilizers and is not necessary. Patients who develop TD owe it to the incompetence of their psychiatrist. A much more important toxicity is the creation of a state of permanent dependence which can be broken only by discontinuing the drug, but then one runs the high risk of allowing the schizophrenia to reappear.

I have referred to the views of leaders of psychiatry today about tranquilizers in the section on housing. Psychiatry has at last realized that patients are not cured by tranquilizers, but they have not yet realized that it is impossible to become normal while on tranquilizers. Several years ago a study was made comparing 100 schizophrenic patients treated at Boston Psychopathic Hospital from 1945 to 1949 with 100 patients treated at the Mental Health Center (the same hospital given a more respectable name) between 1965 and 1969. The pre-tranquilizers group received a combination of psychotherapy, ECT and other treatments then in use. The tranquilizer group received mostly tranquilizers. The outcome was about the same, except that the pre-tranquilizer group was slightly better: they were less dependent on social services. This well-controlled study has received very little attention. It appeared at the height of Establishment euphoria over tranquilizers and was ignored.

Tranquilizers have two main properties: they are therapeutic for psychotic patients; and they make normal people sick. When given to schizophrenic patients, tranquilizers reduce the intensity of perceptual changes. Voices and visions are decreased in intensity and appear less often, and when they do still appear patients are less involved and fearful. Eventually they may go away. However, many chronic patients do not improve at all; their perceptual changes remain untouched. I have examined a large number of chronic patients, using the HOD test after many years of medication, whose HOD perceptual scores remained just as high as before treatment. Tranquilizers also decrease thought disorder but often it is merely weakened. They reduce tension. If depression is a consequence of tension, tranquilizers will be helpful. If depression is primary, tranquilizers may make it worse. Finally, tranquilizers moderate abnormal behavior.

Tranquilizers make normal people sick. They dull the senses, dull the mind and make behavior sluggish. It becomes hard to think, read and reason. Patients may feel their brains are fogged. The tranquilizer syndrome makes it hard to get up in the morning and impossible to carry on any productive employment. Employers will not put up with the sluggish lack of interest generated by the tranquilizers. It is impossible to practice a profession, follow a trade, work in a store, earn a living, run a household effectively, be an artist, fly a plane or pursue any useful occupation.

These two effects of tranquilizers present the tranquilizer therapeutic dilemma.

The aim of treatment is to help patients get well. Tranquilizers start the process very effectively, but as the recovery progress continues and the patient becomes closer to normal, that patient begins to react more and more as any normal person would—becomes sick with the tranquilizer syndrome. At first patients and families are pleased with the result, since the tranquilized state is so much better than the initial psychotic state. Eventually the patient reaches a state where there can be no further improvement; the psychosis has been replaced by the tranquilizer syndrome. The effect of tranquilizers on psychotics and normal subjects is shown in Figure 2. The effect of orthomolecular therapy is shown in Figure 3.

FIGURE 2. *Illustrating the tranquilizer dilemma: the effect of tranquilizers on psychotics and normal subjects*

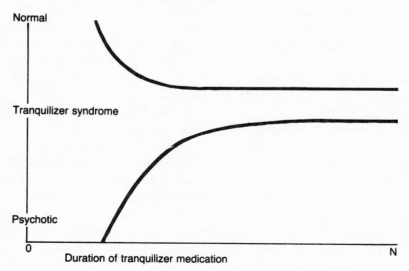

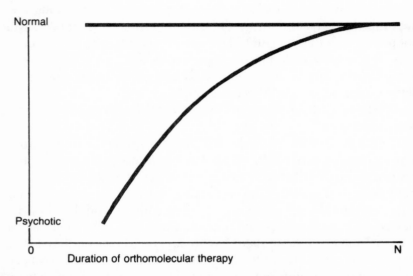

FIGURE 3. *Effect of orthomolecular therapy on psychotic and normal subjects*

Until someone discovers a tranquilizer that does not cause the tranquilizer syndrome, there will be no people normal on tranquilizers.

Attempts have been made to solve this problem by decreasing the dose or by withdrawing the drug. Often there is a sudden surge toward normality as the tranquilizer syndrome disappears. Patients feel much better and families are encouraged. But inevitably in most patients the psychosis returns, forcing the patient back on the tranquilizers again. Patients with the tranquilizer syndrome do not like the effect any more than do normal people who might be tranquilized. Perhaps the only place where normal people are forced to take tranquilizers is in some psychiatric hospitals in Russia where political prisoners are kept. They are just as anxious to escape from the drugged effect as schizophrenics here are. I have an elderly patient in hospital who has been admitted nineteen times for brief admissions because she stopped taking her tranquilizer. The parenteral (injectable) tranquilizers were developed to deal with this problem, but it is very easy to fail to appear for the injection.

On the other hand, nutritional therapy works slowly (except for cerebral allergic patients, who can recover in days), but once it does work continues to do so until patients recover. They do not stop on a plateau somewhere between psychosis and normality. Nutritional therapy does not make normal people sick. The course of orthomolecular treatment for psychotics and normals is shown in Figure 3.

The dilemma is solved by using the best of each treatment. That is, to use tranquilizers for their rapid effect and nutritional therapy to help the patients get well and remain well. This is done by starting treatment with a combination of orthomolecular therapy and the appropriate tranquilizer for patients who require tranquilizers. Many do not, and may be started on nutritional therapy alone. When the combination is used, it is possible to get an effective response using much less tranquilizer, thus avoiding some of the undesirable toxic side effects. As patients begin to respond the treatment is readjusted by decreasing the dose of the drug. If this is done carefully, patients will move steadily toward recovery without stopping at the tranquilizer syndrome level. Eventually they are off tranquilizers or require very small doses. I have several patients who require 1 or 2 mg of Haldol for maintenance. This interferes very little and they are able to function normally. They had required 30 mg when psychotic. Thereafter a few patients learn to use small doses of tranquilizer occasionally, much as people use aspirin to control headache. Orthomolecular therapy combines nutritional and tranquilizer chemicals in such a rational manner.

And if the vitamins and drugs don't do the job, you bring in the shock treatment—sorry, electroconvulsive therapy. It's hard not to think of it as half-electrocuting somebody to make him see it doesn't pay to be crazy. I know it's not that, but it has had a bad press. Can you give me enough information about it to see it more positively?

ECT has been used over the past forty-five years. It is one of the few treatments that has retained its value over such a long period, even though psychiatry underwent massive swings in interest from organic to purely psychological and now back to biological.

But it has also been one of the more controversial treatments in psychiatry. There are a number of reasons for that, the chief one being that it was assessed out of context. In addition, a few highly critical physicians who have not allowed themselves to see its benefits have grossly exaggerated its side effects.

Any medical procedure taken out of context becomes evil. Imagine the reaction of an observer in the operating room for the first time totally unfamiliar with surgery and medicine and the Medical Model. This person would be horrified at the apparent brutality, at the attack of men and women upon a helpless person lying on the table. But once he realized the person on the table is a patient and that doctors and nurses are trying to save his life, the whole procedure becomes entirely different—a human attempt to heal a fellow human being.

A person walking into a room where ECT is being given will also be horrified if he is naive and unaware of the reason for the procedure. But once he is aware, he comes to see that it is a simple, safe procedure which may be life-saving and certainly will save the patient's sanity. This may be more important than life itself.

ECT is never given lightly. It us used when it is the most effective way of saving life and sanity. I will give a few examples.

1. A middle-aged woman was both schizophrenic and alcoholic. She kept her schizophrenia under control by drinking huge amounts of whiskey. Eventually she developed a severe toxic psychosis with some of the characteristics of Wernicke-Korsakov syndrome. Many never recover from this. She was admitted to hospital and went through a very stormy month, but she remained in a very puzzling clinical state. Three psychiatrists including myself, and one neurologist had diagnosed her as suffering from Wernicke-Korsakov disease. She did not respond to thiamine, one of the vitamins used to treat this condition.

    Her behavior gradually became more bizarre, until one day it was evident she was becoming catatonic. In the meantime she had been declared mentally incompetent and her assets were placed in the care of a government administrator. At this time she was started on ECT, receiving four. She was also on niacinamide and small doses of tranquilizer which had been of little use until then. After the fourth treatment she was almost normal. Her estate was returned to her, she was discharged and when seen on follow-up in my office several weeks later, was normal.

Depriving her of alcohol in hospital had gradually allowed her schizophrenia to reappear.

Had she not been given ECT, she would probably have remained psychotic, heavily tranquilized and eventually alienated from her husband whom she had married one year before, from her family and from the community. There was no memory impairment after her ECT. It literally saved her life. Neither she nor her family would ever be critical of ECT. She is still well three years later.

2. A former manic-depressive patient, age 80, living in a nursing home, became depressed. He decided he was dying and therefore refused to eat or drink or to take any medication. He lost weight. I was called to see him and found him lying on the bed, very quiet, emaciated and depressed. He weighed less than 90 pounds and looked like a victim of a Nazi concentration camp.

An ambulance was called and he was admitted to hospital. Intravenous fluid was started immediately and continued for 24 hours each day. I waited a few days to try to rehydrate him. He still refused to eat. I tried to give him ECT but he was so dehydrated that it was impossible to pass any current across his forehead; he would not convulse. Four days later he had his first convulsion. One hour later he had breakfast for the first time in over a month. He had four treatments, got over his depression and remained free of depression until he died of natural causes a year later. ECT saved his life.

3. I treated a young male schizophrenic with orthomolecular therapy. In December he stopped all his vitamins and broke his diet. Over Christmas, during the night, he shot at his parents with a rifle, hitting the pillow between them. He then fled but was captured by the RCMP and charged with attempted murder. On the basis of my evidence he was given a suspended sentence, released under my care to a hospital and there received a series of ECT. He was also on an orthomolecular program. He recovered and remained well;

eventually he married. ECT saved his life and his sanity, and saved him from spending years in a mental hospital, or prison, or both.

4. A young girl in a catatonic state refused to eat or drink. It would have been very difficult and unproductive to have force-fed her. She was given a series of ECT and soon began to eat and drink. ECT saved her from starvation.

These are just a few dramatic examples of how ECT can be therapeutic. Any professional who is opposed to ECT obviously has not seen the results of treatment.

But, like any medical/surgical procedure, ECT has to be used carefully, wisely and for clear indications. When used in this way it remains a useful treatment.

How is ECT given?

Patients walk into the treatment room in the morning without having had breakfast. Before this it has been explained to them and they have signed consent. If they are very psychotic, have no insight and refuse to sign consent, there are several ways of dealing with this. In British Columbia the legal requirement is that a patient has to be certified by two physicians not related to each other. Then the opinion of a second psychiatrist must be obtained. The second psychiatrist arrives at a decision independently of the treating doctor. Once these legal requirements are met the patient will be treated.

In my experience covering thirty-five years, patients have been grateful afterward for ECT and have remained my friends and patients. About fourteen years ago a doctor's son was very sick. One morning at 4 A.M. I received a call from the hospital that my patient was trying to jump out of the window. In fifteen minutes I arrived at the hospital, where I found my agitated, fearful patient surrounded at a safe distance by nurses. I immediately ordered ECT equipment to be set up on the ward. The patient was now violent and the police were called in to help. Two burly policemen arrived. Soon the patient yielded and we gave him his first ECT. Later that morning he had his second. We completed the series. He recovered from his schizophrenia and later became a successful businessman in another city. He and his physician father were very grateful.

The patient lies down on a bed. An anesthetist injects a fast-acting anesthetic containing a muscle relaxant. The patient is asleep in about twenty seconds. When he is properly anesthetized, the current is passed across the forehead. There is a gentle convulsion seen only as a series of tremors. During this time the anesthesist provides oxygen and looks after respiration. The patient comes out of the convulsion in a few minutes and in about half an hour the anesthetic begins to wear off. Nurses watch until the patient is fully awake. Then the patient has something to eat and spends the rest of the day on the ward pursuing usual activities. Usually three treatments per week are given. A series runs everywhere from eight to twenty ECT, depending on the severity of the illness. Most series are under eight.

It is not the aim of ECT to cause amnesia. No one knows why it works. But there will be some amnesia, more pronounced with longer series. In nearly every case memory returns and the patient is not handicapped. However, there may be no memory of the events in hospital at the time ECT was given. Usually this is not a serious problem. Memory loss is greatly reduced if vitamin B3 is taken during and after the treatment. I first noted this in 1952. I was asked to see a patient one month after having been given a series. This patient remained confused and memory was poor. I gave the patient niacin, 1 gram per meal. One month later the patient was normal. The improvement occurred one week after starting the niacin.

ECT is used for two conditions, depression and manic-depressive psychosis in manic state, and schizophrenia. Very few depressions need ECT, as antidepressant medication is usually effective. There are a few, however, who do not respond to drugs or who cannot survive with their deep depression; ECT may bring them out in a few weeks.

Few schizophrenics require ECT. At one time it was widely used: before tranquilizers were developed and after insulin coma had been discontinued. It is used for deeply depressed or very agitated patients who do not respond to medication. It is also used to bring about recovery in patients where other treatment is not helping. I have to give ECT to about ten percent of my schizophrenic patients.

Finally, ECT should not be called "shock therapy." It is electro-convulsive therapy. There is no pain, there is no medical shock and the minimal current used causes no damage to the brain or body. The term "shock" unnecessarily frightens people, as it is incorrect.

CEREBRAL ALLERGY

Dr. Hoffer, you said earlier you would talk about allergies and schizophrenia.

You are right. So far I have referred to that several times. The most important first step is to think about allergies when getting the history of the illness. Allergic reactions often start in infancy, continue throughout childhood and adolescence and into adulthood. The symptoms may vary, but the annoyance and frustration remain.

People become allergic, in most cases, to foods they consume frequently and in large amounts. Cow's milk and sugar are staples for infants not being nursed. These are very common allergies. The baby suffers runny nose, frequent colds, ear ache and infections, tubes in ears, and in my opinion this may lead to enlarged adenoids and tonsils. But even breast-fed babies may become allergic if the mother is drinking large quantities of milk. Many women think they must drink milk to make milk. Infants may become allergic to other foods as well, especially if they are introduced to solid foods too quickly. Colic, abdominal pain, vomiting and diarrhea are common.

I heard a doctor on TV say that children will grow out of their allergies.

This may be based upon the observation that the allergies present in infants do not occur in older children. In fact, there has been a change. Different organ systems are involved. The colds, colic and rashes may leave, to be replaced by behavioral problems, chiefly hyperactivity, and later learning disorders or defects in attention. Other somatic symptoms may start, such as asthma, hay fever or eczema.

Does every person with these allergic reactions become schizophrenic?

Certainly not, but some do. It is essential that these cerebral allergies (a schizophrenic syndrome) be recognized for treatment to be successful.

I assume a dietary history is also important.

Undoubtedly. A history of food likes and dislikes and the type and quantity of foods used must be obtained. People hate foods which make them sick if they know it, but may be very fond of foods they are allergic to. You should suspect any food or food family if it is disliked or consumed to excess. When a patient tells me he drinks eight glasses of milk each day, I promptly suspect milk. Some dislike milk but love cheese; I am one of these. Patients addicted to junk food are much more apt to suffer allergic reactions.

If you suspect certain foods, how can you prove they're implicated?

The most accurate and cheapest way is to use an elimination diet. Many have been described. A four- to seven-day fast is very helpful. The only thing permitted is water, six to eight glasses per day. If the symptoms are gone or much improved by the end of the fast, this is almost proof some allergies are present. However, a fast also clears the digestive tract of yeast (Candida), which may remove symptoms. I have seen patients become free of schizophrenia after a fast and not show any adverse reactions to any foods when tested after the fast. Usually one finds out what the allergenic foods are by eating them, one per meal, after the fast. Those which cause symptoms are then avoided. Children cannot be fasted. For them I use a simple elimination diet, usually milk- and sugar-free for two to four weeks.

I really find it hard to believe foods can be so dangerous for some people.

You and almost every doctor and nutritionist! It must be experienced and seen to be believed. Most patients believe until they have been well a long time. Then they begin to wonder if there was a real connection, or they're intimidated by friends, or even their doctors, who are very skeptical. They will then go back to these foods. A few severe outbreaks of symptoms are very convincing.

Are there any easier ways? Fasting seems to be so unpleasant.

It may be, especially if it is characterized by severe withdrawal symptoms including tension, fatigue, headaches and irritability. Patients should be forewarned about this.

There are simpler, more expensive ways such as sublingual tests, skin tests, cytotoxic blood tests and immunoglobulin assays. All these may be helpful. In my opinion none are as accurate as the elimination diet. Other tests are being developed.

I suppose it is easier to treat when only a few allergies are present?

Much. It is easy to avoid one or two foods, especially ones rarely used. It is more difficult to do so with staples such as wheat or milk. They are ubiquitous in processed foods. One advantage of avoiding sugar is that this leads to a major reduction in the intake of all junk foods.

Occasionally a food will cause an anaphylactic reaction which can cause death. Recently a boy picked up a piece of pastry and asked if it contained peanuts. He was assured it did not. He put it into his mouth, promptly exclaimed, "Oh, no!" and died. This rare, tragic reaction probably can be avoided by large doses of niacin and vitamin C. Dr. E. Boyle, while Director of Research of the Miami Heart Institute, found that niacin protected guinea pigs against anaphylactic shock; an injection of foreign protein into a guinea pig caused no adverse reaction. If the same protein was injected seven days later, it would kill the animal. Guinea pigs pretreated with niacin did not die. The only evidence something was happening was increased nose wiggling.

How can niacin and vitamin C be protective?

Niacin depletes the body of histamine, which is involved in allergic reactions. Niacin depletes histamine so much that there is not enough left to produce a severe reaction. Vitamin C destroys histamine, molecule for molecule. If it is circulating in the blood, histamine will be destroyed as it is dumped into the body. In fact, Dr. F. Klenner used large doses for ameliorating reactions to insect and snake bites. I too have seen how effective vitamin C can be in quickly eliminating hives caused by a hornet sting. It should react as well against poison ivy.

If I suffered from a deadly allergic reaction, I would certainly want to protect myself by taking both niacin and vitamin C, and would carry with me an emergency kit containing adrenalin and antihistamines.

Allergic patients must be paranoid about foods and eat only when they know how that food has been prepared.

Must the elimination diet be followed for very long?

That depends on the person and whether the allergy is fixed or variable. A variable reaction will disappear in time, and that food may be eaten if this is done infrequently and in moderate amounts.

But six months or more of abstinence may be needed after a person is well. I suggest sticking to the diet for at least six months. Then they can test each of the forbidden foods, but not at the same time. If the reaction does not recur, that food may be used sparingly, every few days. If the reaction does recur, it may be a fixed allergy—it will never go away. I have a fixed allergy to dairy products.

What do you recommend for people who have many food allergies?

Treatment for these people is more complicated and requires dedication by the person. The best way is to follow the rotation diets which have been published. Books by Dr. Marshall Mandell, for example, are very good. After the diet is understood and followed, the allergic reactions should slowly ease away. The body is able to accommodate to foods provided it is not bombarded daily. If diets alone are not helpful, one can try anti-allergy preparations such as antihistamines or Intal (sodium cromoglycate), a semi-synthetic derivative of bioflavonoids, or tricyclic antidepressants.

Can schizophrenics recover if their allergies are not dealt with?

That's very unlikely. Some of my most difficult patients have refused to follow the anti allergy part of treatment, either because they would not, or could not, or were not supported by family or professional staff.

I recall a patient I saw in 1952, admitted because he could not urinate—for no physical reason. He was a paranoid schizophrenic. He was started on niacin, soon recovered and remained well for the next five years. Then he stopped the niacin, relapsed within two years and was started on tranquilizers by a psychiatrist who believed giving vitamins was quackery. A few years later he was referred to me. He no longer responded to any treatment, including ECT, and eventually I had to commit him to a mental hospital. No one could cope with his psychotic behavior. After several years in hospital he once more could not urinate. He was transferred to City Hospital for investigation. Again no reason was found and I was asked to see him.

Knowing he had not responded to anything, I asked him if he would do a four-day fast. He agreed. On the fifth day he was normal. He was free of all hallucinations, was not fearful or paranoid, and his mood was good. He was then given a glass of milk. Within half an hour he was violently ill with nausea and vomiting, severe diarrhea, abdominal cramps. This lasted all day. The next morning I told him he had a milk allergy. To my surprise, he replied he had known this for many years. Then he surprised me even more. He said he would never stop drinking milk and that he no longer wanted to see me. When I asked him why, he said he saw no alternative to remaining psychotic because this provided him shelter and care, and he would not have to face the responsibilities of normal living. Another psychiatrist was called in. He restarted the patient's tranquilizers and shipped him back to the mental hospital, where he died two years later from leukemia.

The presence of cerebral allergies must complicate research.

Enormously, for one can be sure that any large group of patients will be a mixed batch of the schizophrenic syndrome. If two doctors in different cities study groups of, say, fifty patients, in one a small fraction may have cerebral allergy, in the second a much larger group. In our early double-blind controlled studies in the 1950s, we found the niacin used alone did not help chronic patients, but did help acute ones. Probably our acute population had few cerebral allergies while our chronic population had many.

The two major research groups who claimed they had repeated our studies got mixed results. The New Jersey group under Dr. J. Wittenborn confirmed us: his chronic patients did not respond, his acute patients did. The Montreal group under Dr. T. Ban, who worked for Dr. H. Lehmann, used mostly chronics, but denied this by labelling them "early admissions," wanting to leave the impression that they were acute. They were not. The American Psychiatric Association Task Force Report chaired by Dr. M. Lipton drew heavily on the Montreal work and ignored the New Jersey studies. Thus they found it simple to claim that megavitamin therapy was of no value for any schizophrenics.

You must have brought this to the attention of the American Psychiatric Association.

Yes. They ignored it. They knew most psychiatrists would assume they had conducted scientific studies and so could be trusted to draw scientific conclusions. Most psychiatrists were not motivated enough to read all the original papers. Linus Pauling did. He concluded the A.P.A. was wrong.

But you do treat chronic schizophrenics. Many of your examples are of chronic patients.

Yes, but we now know much more. When the entire spectrum of orthomolecular treatment is used, the results with chronics are very good, but not quite as good as they are for early, acute patients. One must use nutrition, necessary supplements in optimum doses, and the whole program I have been describing in this book.

In your opinion, how many of acute and chronic populations are cerebral-allergic?

First, I'd better make clear what I mean by acute schizophrenics. They are the discontinuous type, patients who have shown a capacity to recover without specific treatment or recover quickly with ortho-molecular treatment. They are patients who have suffered one or more episodes. If we apply the orthomolecular spectrum of treatment for at least two years, around ninety percent will be well or much improved, and the rest will be better. None will have been made worse.

Chronic patients are those who have not shown any improvement before starting on this treatment program. The orthomolecular approach, with more emphasis on allergy treatment, will over five years bring fifty percent to being well or much improved. Many chronic patients will not respond to any treatment because they are brain-damaged or psychologically damaged from too many years of illness and all the psychosocial handicaps it has produced. They will need permanent care or asylum.

ACCEPTANCE

Your approach, effective as it seems to be, obviously isn't the standard one. Has it had any sort of wide acceptance?

There are now about 200 members of the Academy of Orthomolecular Psychiatry, accredited physicians who among them have treated more than 50,000 patients. Several hospitals in the United States use orthomolecular treatment for mental patients, including schizophrenics, including Bryce Hospital in Tuscaloosa, Alabama, where Dr. Osmond, with whom I developed this approach, is on the staff.

I will say that there is a lot of opposition still to the orthomolecular approach—most modern psychiatric departments, for reasons it doesn't do any good to speculate on, show a determined avoidance of any interest in nutritional treatment. I had an experience some years ago which illustrates both the strength of this opposition—to my mind, irrational—and the hopeful prospect of its weakening. At that time, the government of Alberta in response to pressure from its citizens appointed a commission to investigate the theory and practice of orthomolecular psychiatry. None of the three commissioners was friendly. One, a professor of psychiatry, had a strong psychological orientation during his entire professional career. He consistently lectured to his students about the evils of orthomolecular psychiatry, grossly exaggerating the side effects and ruling out any beneficial effect. Once he reported me to the College of Physicians and Surgeons because I was sending out form letters containing information about vitamins to North American people. He accused me of practicing psychiatry by mail. The charge was so patently absurd that the College, after my explanation, quickly dropped the matter. Another member of the committee was a pediatrician, the most impartial member, and the chairman, a professor of pharmacology, had gone on record in the public press the year before that the whole matter of using vitamins for psychiatric patients was nonsense. In my opinion they were as biased and unfit to enquire into this matter as the American Psychiatric Association Task Force on Orthomolecular Psychiatry and Megavitamins under the chairmanship of Professor Morris Lipton had been. I refused to appear at their hearings. The chairman approached me personally and agreed to come to Saskatoon to speak to me privately. Their conclusion was much more favorable than I expected. The evidence they had collected had been powerful enough to overwhelm their initial antagonism and move them to urge some positive courses.

We, therefore, RECOMMEND that adequate financial support be provided for well-designed and controlled clinical trials of megavitamin therapy, as judged by a process of scientific peer review.

We RECOMMEND that strong encouragement be given to research into mechanisms underlying clinical disorders for which megavitamin therapy is now advocated on empirical grounds.

Therefore, we RECOMMEND that collaboration between proponents of megavitamin therapy and other investigators, qualified in the field of clinical investigation, be encouraged in the design and execution of future clinical trials of megavitamin therapy.

To this end, we RECOMMEND that qualified medical investigators who are proponents of megavitamin therapy be welcomed to carry out controlled clinical trials at hospitals under university auspices, in collaboration with other medical investigators not committed to the megavitamin hypothesis.

Hospitals and Medical Professionals

Dr. Hoffer, I preferred to be at home when I was being treated. Do other patients respond better if treated at home?

The best place in which to be treated is one's own home, and this is possible in most cases. There are many advantages, such as being in familiar surroundings, having family around and privacy. However, many patients are too sick to be treated at home. They have to be admitted to a hospital if they are suicidal or homicidal, or so disturbed that normal people can not tolerate their behavior. It is important not to force families to cope with psychotic behavior too long. Their tolerance level may break, and when the patient is finally admitted they may refuse to take them back after discharge.

Several years ago, a very sick adolescent girl was admitted as an emergency case to my hospital in Victoria. She had set fire to the curtains in her home on two occasions, had been seen in a forensic clinic, diagnosed antisocial and blacklisted by every psychiatric ward and mental hospital in Vancouver. Following her second fire episode she was kept in jail for a week as no psychiatric ward would take her. After she began to recover from her severe schizophrenia it became clear that her father did not want her back, or at least was so fearful of her behavior that he could not tolerate allowing her to come home, nor did her mother want her at home. Only after several visits in hospital after she was improved did she go home. Now the relationship is good. Had she been forced to stay at home when she was psychotic, I doubt she would be allowed to come back home when improved, and her future would have been jeopardized. She is now well on the way to recovery.

Ideally a home should provide privacy, shelter, good food, freedom and good family support, but psychiatrists have no control over the homes their patients come from.

The impact of not providing a home can be devastating. One result was the near-assassination of President Reagan. John Hinckley's psychiatrist advised his parents to send him on his way. This was the beginning of his fateful journey to St. Elizabeth's Hospital, where he will probably spend the rest of his life tranquilized but unable to function or get well. Too often my patients' parents have been advised to throw out their sick sons or daughters because they were "lazy." On tranquilizers alone at the doses required, *most* patients appear lazy.

Yet I did appreciate being in a hospital when I was very depressed.

Hospitals protect both the patient and the community. The best hospitals follow the golden rule of medicine, not to do the patient harm. The worst hospitals keep the patient sick and add to his burden the results of being in an institution too long.

Psychiatric patients may be treated in general hospitals alongside physically sick patients or in psychiatric wards or mental hospitals which are entirely psychiatric. They provide protection to the patient, shelter, nursing care, nutrition, occupational therapy and rehabilitation. In short, they do all those things which must be done for patients to get well. They vary in quality of housing from government-operated mental hospitals to very expensive private hospitals which cost up to $100,000 per year. The best hospitals are small. Very large hospitals become dehumanizing.

Psychiatric hospitals have a very bad reputation. I heard they were even worse many years ago.

In 1950, when I first entered psychiatry, most North American hospitals were very bad. Patients were crowded into rundown wards with no privacy. They were short of staff and tranquilizers had yet to appear. Patients were segregated by sex. These hospitals were totally inadequate. In order to persuade governments to improve these hospitals, relatives and friends of the patients were invited to visit as often as possible and to make their views about the hospital known to their governments. In order to help them evaluate the quality of the hospital, F. H. Kahan wrote a booklet for the Canadian Schizophrenia Foundation called *How to Judge a Mental Hospital*. Every family should have this booklet in their possession so they can judge how well the hospital housing their relative is doing. (Canadian Schizophrenia Foundation, 2229 Broad Street, Regina, Saskatchewan, S4P 1Y7.)

These inadequate institutions fueled the movement to move patients out of the hospitals into the community. The move was sponsored by a small group of "community psychiatrists," assisted legally by civil libertarians who believed that patient rights were infringed upon. The move to discharge patients became a stampede. I can recall visiting medical superintendants in their offices and seeing large charts on their walls showing the number of patients by year. The graphs plunged steeply downward. There was competition to see which hospital could discharge patients most rapidly. They had forgotten that it is possible to empty any hospital simply by writing a discharge order only if one ignores the patient and the community. A recent review in the *New York Times* (November 7, 1984) outlines the history of this mass exodus from large institutions into the streets. What happened was that chronic schizophrenic patients, whose behavior was such that society could not tolerate it, were converted into chronic patients whose behavior was marginally better on tranquilizers, so that they could be said to be no danger to themselves or to the community. Danger to the community was interpreted narrowly as homicidal danger, but no one considered another danger—the danger to the social structure of the community and the destruction of parts of the inner core of the major North American cities. There is now a backlash; psychiatrists who could not be restrained in their eagerness to empty the hospitals are now complaining bitterly over the failure of the present program.

How did the reform movement get started?

It all began with a World Health Organization report which recommended that mental hospitals should not exceed a capacity of 300 because larger hospitals became very unwieldy, but this idea was not original with this report. Before 1910, shortly after Saskatchewan became a province of Canada, it became necessary to find a place to house the mentally ill. The young government invited an American psychiatrist to survey the problem and recommend what they should do. He recommended a series of small hospitals. However, the Toronto architects retained to design the hospital refused to follow his advice. They claimed it would be too costly to heat individual cottages or buildings and instead designed one building to house 1000 patients. By 1950 it housed twice as many.

When I joined the Department of Public Health of Saskatchewan in 1950 to become Director of Psychiatric Research, Dr. D. G. McKerracker, Director of the Psychiatric Services Branch, wanted to bring Saskatchewan's two mental hospitals into the twentieth century. He read the W.H.O. report on mental hospitals and adapted it to the situation in Saskatchewan. With the help of Dr. S. Lawson and Dr. H. Osmond he formulated the Saskatchewan Plan, as it became known. The idea was to divide Saskatchewan into seven regions, each containing a modern psychiatric hospital. In each region families would not need to travel farther than fifty miles to visit their relatives; *i.e.*, each region had a radius of one hour (fifty miles). Patients would be treated in these hospitals as before and discharged when they were fit to be discharged. They were not meant merely to be first-aid stations for the mentally ill.

But the objectives of the Saskatchewan Plan seem to have gotten lost somewhere.

Two striking developments soon changed the main objective of the Saskatchewan Plan. One, the introduction of tranquilizers, made psychiatrists overly optimistic about the effect on their patients; they assumed that damping down the symptoms was the same as a cure and ignored the warnings of a few farsighted British psychiatrists. One of them, Dr. Meyer-Gross, declared that treating schizophrenics with tranquilizers replaced one psychosis with another. With tranquilizers it was possible to bring patients under control very quickly and to discharge them in a few weeks rather than a few years. If the patients remained on the medication, they could be cared for at home. This shifted the burden from the mental hospital onto the family and the community.

Community psychiatry was the second development. Psychiatrists believed that any community, no matter how bad, was better than any institution, no matter how good. At the same time they maintained the contradictory view that schizophrenia arose from family, social and community pressure. I am still surprised at their ability to maintain two contradictory views at the same time. They persuaded governments that money could be saved by discharging patients and providing alternative resources in the community. These ideas became widespread in the U.S.A. and Canada, leading to our present dismal situation.

Richard D. Lyons, in his *New York Times* report, truthfully wrote, "The policy that led to the release of most of the nation's mentally ill patients from the hospital to the community is now widely regarded as a major failure," and "sweeping critiques of the policy, notably the recent report of the American Psychiatric Association, have spread the blame everywhere, faulting politicians, civil libertarian lawyers and psychiatrists." The APA report apparently did not blame itself, yet the APA encouraged the move to empty the hospitals. Lyons continues, "The picture is one of cost-conscious policy makers who were quick to buy optimistic projections that were, in some instances, buttressed by misinformation and a willingness to suspend skepticism."

Lyons is unaware of the role played by Saskatchewan, which led the movement but did not allow it to move as fast in Saskatchewan. Three Saskatchewan psychiatrists were leaders in the community psychiatry movement. All three, Dr. J. Cumming, Dr. H. Lafave and Dr. F. Greenberg, were invited by New York State to move to Albany under Dr. Miller, then Commissioner for Psychiatry. There was a rapid acceleration of the discharge of patients from huge institutions to the streets of New York City. When Governor Nelson Rockefeller was replaced, so was Commissioner Miller, and the three

Canadians came home, but the movement did not cease. It is not coincidental that the backlash became strongest in New York with many critical articles in the *New York Times*. The original Saskatchewan Plan became corrupted into a policy of deinstitutionalization for its own sake.

Lyons writes, "Politicians were dogged by the image and financial problems posed by the state hospitals and that the scientific and medical establishment sold congress and the state legislatures a quick fix for a complicated problem that was bought sight unseen."

Dr. John A. Talbot, President of the APA, is quoted as saying, "The psychiatrists involved in the policy making at that time certainly oversold community treatment and our credibility today is probably damaged because of it. . . . Policies were based partly on wishful thinking." Dr. Talbot seems unaware that even by 1960 it was clear the community psychiatry philosophy was inappropriate, had been oversold on the virtues of living in a community and depended almost entirely on the chemical restraint made possible by tranquilizers. Experience in English hospitals which had been opened for years suggested caution. Both Dr. Osmond and I warned of the consequences of depending on these drugs, but no one was listening. Italy has just gone well into a similar program even though it is now realized that it does much more harm than good.

The original policy, based upon a misguided alteration of the Saskatchewan Plan, was "backed by scores of national and professional organizations and several hundred people prominent in medicine, academia and politics." Dr. M. Brewster Smith, Vice President of the Joint Commission on Mental Illness and Health, said the Commission supported the movement because it was oversold. "Extravagant claims were made for the benefits of shifting from state hospitals to community clinics." C. Schlaefer, Secretary-Treasurer of the Joint Commission, is quoted as saying that "he was now disgusted with the advice presented by leading psychiatrists. . . . Tranquilizers became the panacea for the mentally ill. . . . The state programs were buying them by the carload, sending the drugged patients back to the community and the psychiatrists never tried to stop this. Local mental health centers were going to be the greatest thing going, but no one wanted to think it through."

Dr. Bertram S. Brown, Director, National Institute of Mental

Health, shaped the community center legislation in 1963. He now says, "Yes, the doctors were overpromising for the politicians. The doctors did not believe that community care would cure schizophrenia and we did allow ourselves to be somewhat misrepresented." He neglects to say he had a very influential position and could have insisted that more research and thought were needed. At the time he did not publicly voice any doubt about the program. Lyons writes, "In the thousands of pages of testimony before Congressional committees in the late 1950s and early 1960s, little doubt was expressed about the wisdom of deinstitutionalization." Dr. Braceland, former president of the APA, said that "we had no alternative to the use of drugs for schizophrenia." He was, in fact, aware of the use of nutrition and vitamins but, like most psychiatrists, totally ignored our work.

Dr. Frank R. Lipton and Dr. A. Sabatini of Bellevue pointed to a major flaw in the program. This was "the notion that serious chronic mental disorders could be minimized, if not totally prevented, through care provided within the local community. This shift in thinking was not adequately validated, yet it became one of the major conceptual bases for moving the locus of care."

Dr. Loren Mosher, for a while head of the Schizophrenia Section of NIMH, was always in favor of community care. He published several studies "showing" that schizophrenics in homes did as well as those in hospital. He made little reference to the fact that neither did very well. He was one of the psychiatrists very enthusiastic about the Italian development, which is doing twenty years later what North America did in 1965. Dr. Mosher did not believe there is such a disease as schizophrenia, which made him an appropriate first director of the Schizophrenia Section of NIMH.

Every psychiatrist, Lyons reported in his *Times* article, now pleads a simple error, but they appear to blame others. They all now agree with Mr. Jack R. Ewalt that drugs "are just another treatment, not a magic."

They blame the state governments for not adequately funding community care centers.

The community psychiatry program was adopted so hastily because psychiatrists oversold the virtues of the program, overestimated the therapeutic efficacy of the tranquilizers, promised governments they would save money, and ignored the persons most affected: the patients, their families and the community. Had they followed the original Saskatchewan Plan, they would have recommended the construction of a number of small regional hospitals which would eventually have replaced the large mental hospitals, but would have remained hospitals, not community mental health centers. Had they taken our vitamin work more seriously and conducted the therapeutic studies needed to convince skeptical psychiatrists, they could have solved the problem. Patients would have been kept in hospital until they were well enough to cope. This would have markedly reduced the readmission rate and greatly reduced the need for hospital beds.

Will we always need asylums—safe havens for many sick patients?

For many chronic schizophrenics and for brain-damaged patients we will need asylums, permanent homes or shelters, where they can live in decent surroundings. These asylums could be surrounded by smaller special homes supervised by the hospital to ensure they are not abused and mistreated. These homes would be satellite mini hospitals.

Families of the patients living in these homes would set up committees whose job it would be to protect their relatives and to ensure decent, humane care. They would report to an ombudsman who would keep the director or superintendent of the hospital complex informed and would enforce action.

One of the hospitals I was in believed in a "therapeutic milieu" as the only valid treatment. It clearly isn't, but is it any good at all?

The therapeutic value of hospitals must not be overstated. For many years community psychiatrists followed the notion that there was something therapeutic about living in groups. This became known as the "therapeutic milieu." A cynical lawyer once described this as the right to inhale the smelly air of the hospital. Hospitals without treatment are not therapeutic. The best examples were all the mental hospitals in existence in 1950. They were monstrous, huge, inhuman warehouses for the unfortunate afflicted mentally ill. Dr. Humphry Osmond has stated that if anyone wanted to design and operate a hospital whose sole purpose was to make and keep people sick, one would design any one of the hospitals then in existence. A hospital without treatment is not a hospital, it is a monstrous institution. Of all the factors essential to get people well, treatment is the most important, but all variables must be provided for in the best and most economical mix.

For many years, while psychiatrists tried to reform the hospitals, governments were very reluctant to provide funds. Every hospital demanded more and more money to provide more and more staff, psychiatrists, nurses, psychologists, social workers and others. There was a continual tug-of-war between governments, who were being pressed by the public to do more and who in turn pressed their medical civil servants to do better, and these psychiatrists who demanded more money. Every time the public criticized the hospitals, their superintendents would demand more money. It never occurred to them to try more effective treatments. They already had the cure, tranquilizers, and merely needed staff to carry out all the psychosocial therapies of which they were so fond.

How would you compare the relative importance of hospital and the treatment used?

In the 1960s I conducted an experiment to measure the relative importance of housing and treatment in helping schizophrenic patients. A comparison had been made by Dr. Colin Smith, my deputy director of psychiatric research, of treatment at the University Hospital psychiatric department and at the closest mental hospital, ninety miles away. This was a rigorous study. The daily cost at the University Hospital was about $80 per day while at the mental hospital it was perhaps one-third of that. Costs are relevant, as they represent staff. University Hospital had professors of psychiatry, residents and students, providing one doctor for every four to five patients. The mental hospital provided about one physician for every 100 patients. The results of treatment in both hospitals were identical.

My study was an extension of this idea. A new nursing home had just been constructed in Saskatoon. It was built on the style of a motel, with individual bedrooms, a dining room, lounge, and so on. It was operated by a few nurses and other staff. At that time there were hardly any places in the United States where patients could go for treatment and vitamins. I was receiving hundreds of letters each week from people seeking help. Many wanted to come to Saskatoon, but I could not overload the psychiatric ward with non-residents. The nursing home agreed to house these patients for $20 per day. For this they received a decent, clean, single room, medication under nursing supervision, good food and freedom to use the home and its facilities. I was the psychiatrist in charge. We also used electroconvulsive therapy (ECT) with a nurse and the head of the department of anesthesia of one of the hospitals.

The patients I admitted to this nursing home were all chronic schizophrenics who had not responded to treatment with tranquilizers, either as outpatients or in mental hospitals in the United States and Canada. My objectives were to find out: could these very sick schizophrenics be treated in a nursing home which provided shelter, food and minimum nursing care but which did not provide any psychologists, social workers, group therapy, recreational and rehabilitation therapy? And what would be the results of treatment? After treating about a hundred patients I concluded that they could be treated in simple nursing homes, provided the right care was used. There were very few episodes of aggression or other undesirable acts, certainly no more than were experienced in the University Hospital. The second question was also answered positively. The results of treatment were better than those obtained by University Hospital or by any of the previous hospitals. Out of one hundred former treatment failures, at least 50 percent were much better after treatment.

I concluded that with proper treatment, housing costs could be reduced to one-quarter. The patients paid $20 per day at the nursing home; at University Hospital they would have paid $80 per day.

In order of priority, treatment is first, followed by the hospital and the care it provides. If I have a choice of providing the best hospital with no treatment, or the worst hospital with orthomolecular treatment, I would select the latter. Ideally, one should have the best of both.

One can compare the results of treatment in any one of the best private psychiatric institution in the U.S.A. to the results obtained by Coral Ridge Psychiatric Hospital, which provided a comprehensive orthomolecular treatment program. It successfully treats 85 percent of its chronic schizophrenic patients. Other private hospitals do not publish their treatment results, but as they depend only on tranquilizers it is unlikely that they help more than ten percent.

Some of the patients who were in hospital with me were too sick to live independently and not sick enough for the hospital. What do you recommend for them?

Alternative homes vary in size and function, falling somewhere between mental hospitals and private homes. Large nursing homes would be more like the hospitals while small homes housing four or so patients would be closer to the private homes. Communities will have a number of each. Generally, the sickest patients are housed in the nursing homes and have the worst prognosis. Patients more likely to recover are housed in the smaller units. In Victoria, B.C., there are individual apartments and homes housing improved patients. Several of my patients who require minimal supervision live in such places. They are cared for by social welfare and have access to social workers for support. Many will eventually move into the community as independent citizens.

All these homes must provide the same standards of care, decent, humane surroundings with shelter, good food, privacy and support. They should also provide a stimulating environment for patients ready for social interaction.

The best homes are managed by warm, tough, dedicated professionals or private entrepreneurs. They are interested in helping their guests become well. These fortunate homes need little outside supervision. Other homes may need a good deal of supervision to prevent exploitation. Basically, it is the duty of the treating psychiatrists to ensure that the patients are not abused and exploited.

An ideal system will contain various types of housing to provide homes for every type of patient. Such a system can be illustrated by a number of concentric rings and two-way arrows.

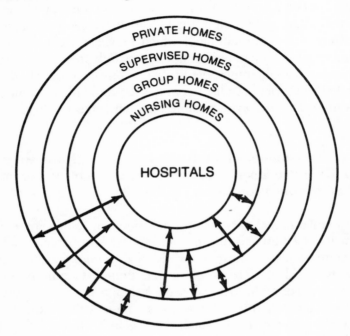

There are ten types of interaction. In any effective system there will be a ready exchange between housing units. If a nursing home—or any other home—is forced to keep a disturbed patient too long, it will not take that patient back. There may be a limit of 48 hours. It is more economical to admit these patients quickly and have a place for them to go back to rather than to force a home to keep them beyond endurance and then have the patient in hospital for months because it takes time to find a place.

So many chronic patients live on the streets as bag ladies, drifters and derelicts. Is it possible they can be treated without a proper shelter?

There is no treatment on the streets. In the term "street" I include rundown hotels, hostels, private homes and any housing which fails to provide shelter, good food, decent care and privacy. I also include cardboard boxes, caves under bridges, sewers, street grates, as well as institutions not designed to treat such patients, such as the Library of Congress in Washington, D.C., which, as already mentioned, has become the day room for St. Elizabeth's Hospital.

It is inhumane, degrading and totally inappropriate to use the street as a treatment milieu, but that is the result of the policy of emptying our mental hospitals without providing a community network of housing and support services. A bad community is no better than a bad hospital, both are equally undesirable.

Using the streets as a treatment facility has destroyed some of the central areas of most large cities. Discharged patients are forced to live in what rundown places they can afford. It is easier to justify paying money for patients in hospital, even a bad hospital, than to pay money if it is called welfare. They rent rooms with minimal, if any, cooking facilities. They are preyed upon by unscrupulous individuals, and they prey upon others. Normal families in such an area move out, and the process of degradation of the community accelerates. Crime, usually petty crime, goes up markedly. When arrested, former patients are not allowed back into hospitals and find themselves in jail. Over ten percent of all inmates are mentally ill. The prison system is forced to cope with a population of sick people it has not been designed to help. Some prisons have taken over empty mental hospitals and are filling them with mentally sick prisoners. Perhaps the same patients, discharged from a hospital, are now back in the same building. However, the psychiatric division of the state can be proud of its ability to close down that hospital while the prison system is forced to reopen it under a new budget and regime.

A few dedicated individuals have been moved to do something. On November 4, 1984, "Sixty Minutes" described what Mitch Snyder was doing in Washington, D.C. Washington houses St. Elizabeth's Hospital, which at one time was to have been the prototype of the enlightened hospital of the future. Mr. Snyder operates a shelter for the homeless. He took over an empty building to make it a shelter and resisted an attempt by the government to close him down. He refuses government money because of the restrictions this would impose. He stated that 50 percent of the residents were there as a result of deinstitutionalization. The television showed classic examples of chronic schizophrenics. On seeing this show, I was reminded of the Saskatchewan Hospital at Weyburn, Saskatchewan, in 1950. It was then considered one of the three worst mental hospitals in the world by Dr. John Weir, Medical Director of the Rockefeller Foundation.

In thirty-five years we have come full circle, from totally inadequate mental hospitals which warehoused patients to totally inadequate street institutions which provide even less care. In 1950 the large institutions provided minimal care but protected the community from the mentally ill and the consequences of psychotic behavior. The present street institutions provide even less care and no longer protect patients, families and the community. A well-known television ad for electric shavers proclaims that one cutting edge cuts hair incredibly close, the second even closer. We can now say that our 1950 mental hospitals provided incredibly bad care, our present street institutions provide care even worse. A century and more ago, Dorothea Lynde Dix sparked the first movement to bring the mentally ill out of the inhumane Bedlams of the time. We need her back.

In the hospital I was seen by so many different sorts of professionals that I lost track. Just who does what?

Schizophrenics are treated by psychiatrists and general practitioners. In Canada, patients are referred to psychiatrists by their G.P. This has many advantages over accepting patients directly—without referral. Patients who are referred have already had a physical examination and common problems will have diagnosed and treated. Thus the psychiatrist need not be as concerned about the usual physical problems. Psychiatrists in Canada do not do physical or neurological examinations. However, being originally trained as physicians, we should always be aware that physical disease can cause psychiatric symptoms. It would be irresponsible to neglect a physical disease just because the G.P. has missed it. When such a condition is discovered, the referring G.P. is alerted and expected to treat it.

Physicians have spent four years in medical school, have graduated and have interned for at least one year. They can then practice or take additional training to become a specialist. Psychiatry is one of the specialties. To become a psychiatrist, the physician accepts a residency in a psychiatric treatment center and spends four years in Canada, three in the United States, in postgraduate training.

If the Canadian passes the exams set by the Royal College of Physicians and Surgeons, s/he is awarded a fellowship (F.R.C.P.S. Can.), and is now entitled to practice psychiatry after the provincial licensing requirements are met. In the U.S.A. the resident after three years must take another year in practicing psychiatry and then write the "Boards." The psychiatric training is very similar in Canada and the United States.

A psychologist is not an M.D. but has gone through college to achieve a B.S. in psychology, later an M.S. and finally, if all the requirements are completed, a Ph.D. Psychologists can be called doctor, as can all Ph.D.'s, but they are not allowed to mislead the public into believing they are medical doctors. Psychologists are not allowed to write prescriptions, do surgery, practice medicine or make medical diagnoses. They are allowed to do psychotherapy and may be more skillful at it than psychiatrists. Psychologists may be called on to test patients and advise doctors and others about their conclusions.

Because of the nature of their training, psychologists are mostly interested in psychosocial factors and much less in biological or physical problems.

Psychologists are neither inferior nor superior to psychiatrists. They are different, and perform different functions. Many patients confuse psychologists and psychiatrists, and a few psychologists do not bother to correct this error. Also, many psychiatrists have moved so far from the Medical Model that they are practicing psychology.

Psychiatrists are given the right to practice medicine and psychiatry, which is a branch of medicine. They must also accept responsibility for treatment. They earn more money than psychologists, and just as often earn less than other medical specialties.

Psychiatrists vary enormously in their approach to psychiatric practice. This range of variation is much greater than it is for any other specialty. All dermatologists will treat skin disorders in a standardized way. They will differ in diagnostic skill and experience, but essentially they all use identical treatments. All peptic ulcers are given the same diet and the same drugs. One internist is much like any other in his practice. Obstetricians deliver babies more or less using the same techniques. But psychiatrists vary from psychoanalysts, who have forgotten there is a body, to tranquilizer psychiatrists who have forgotten that there is a person with psychosocial problems. As in any frequency distribution, the extremes occur rarely. When it comes to psychotherapy there are over 200 variants, and this diversity of interests and skills is puzzling to patients.

Patients have freedom of choice of specialists with two exceptions: if they are in a coma and not able to decide; and if they are committed to a mental hospital. With no other specialty are patients obliged to take doctors assigned to them.

Psychiatric patients are treated in private hospitals, public psychiatric hospitals operated by general hospitals or governments and public mental hospitals owned and managed by governments. In private hospitals patients know who their psychiatrists are. In teaching hospitals patients often do not know who their doctors are. They are visited by a succession of people who are called doctor: from fourth-year medical students to interns to first, second, third and fourth year residents to the professor theoretically in charge. If they do not know who their doctor is, the Medical Model is so attenuated as to have lost its meaning. I do not think a patient can be a patient to a group of fledgling doctors with final responsibility resting in a doctor he may never see, the Professor. I have asked patients who their doctor was after they had been in a university hospital for several weeks and found them unable to tell me because they had had so many doctors deal with them.

In mental hospitals patients have no choice of doctors; if there is a mismatch, too bad, and because these psychiatrists are responsible to the institution, patients may come second. No matter how they behave, their patients cannot fire them. Psychiatric nurses are nurses with additional training in nursing psychiatric patients. Nurses do not diagnose, nor do they prescribe treatment. They must observe, record the patient's progress in the hospital, provide nursing care and carry out orders given by the psychiatrist. Good nurses will bring important aspects of behavior to the psychiatrist's attention. They will also make treatment recommendations which should be considered seriously by the psychiatrist. Nurses listen to patients and calm and support them. It is not their function to do psychotherapy, nor to interfere in the treatment program being followed by the psychiatrist in charge. Nurses in general hospitals wear uniforms, nurses in psychiatric wards do not. This idea arose thirty years ago when psychiatrists were abandoning the Medical Model. They had concluded that nurses' uniforms acted as a barrier between them and the patients. Perhaps it did for some, but I have never heard any of my patients complain about their nurse's uniform—when they still wore them. On the contrary, the change at first made it hard for some to tell nurses from patients. This would be especially difficult for patients who were confused or delirious.

I have found that the nurse's attitude toward a patient, even toward difficult ones, is to a large degree colored by the psychiatrist's attitude. This is not surprising, as they are part of the treatment team.

I was never sure of the difference between social workers and psychologists.

Social workers are trained to deal with social problems arising from the social environment. They may take intake histories, *i.e.*, speak to relatives and other people to obtain past history, family history, etc. They also help in finding homes for the homeless, jobs for the jobless. They act as a link between the psychiatric hospital and community agencies whose help is required. They do not do psychotherapy or prescribe treatment.

Psychologists do not have a medical degree and therefore cannot legally write prescriptions. Clinical psychologists are trained to give psychotherapy and may do this better than psychiatrists. Psychologists also do tests, counsel and may be part of a clinical therapeutic team. They may have any graduate degree up to a Ph.D.

Don't some patients find it hard to tell these professionals apart?

In a few psychiatric wards these professionals have been confused. In one unit at a university department all members of the treatment team were considered equal and the head of the team could be anyone. However, when it came to writing prescriptions one was "more equal": the psychologist or social worker in charge would advise which drug should be used and the M.D. would be asked to write the prescription.

I know you emphasize the importance of good food and optimum nutrition. Is this provided in our hospitals?

General hospitals pay little attention to the nutritional quality of the food they serve. One cannot blame the hospital; the doctor in charge of each patients should be responsible. I am not saying hospitals pay no attention to food, but they pay attention to the cosmetic qualities of food: is it served warm? are the colors balanced? are the food rules followed? They have no objection to serving junk food in abundance. Fresh fruit is rarely served. Patients should demand they not be charged for food and have their meals catered instead. Ideally, hospitals should follow the six main food rules I describe later (page 130), but they do not. The evidence is apparent to anyone who has been a patient in a hospital and knows something about food.

Recently, a member of my family was treated for a broken hip as an emergency at Bellevue Hospital in New York City. The surgery was superb and the outcome good. The food was atrocious; her first meal consisted of cold chicken soup, a bottle of ginger ale, a piece of white bread and a jellied dessert. For the entire week she was there this was the quality of the food—junk. I brought food in and provided her with essential vitamins. The nursing staff considered vitamins more dangerous than drugs. Why couldn't a hospital provide as good nutritional treatment as it does surgical treatment?

Dr. W. Steffe, Director, Department of Medicine, St. Vincent's Hospital and Health Center, said, "Hospitals are malnutrition centers." Ten percent of all patients in hospitals are in a severe state of malnutrition and are at risk for other complications such as infection and surgical wounds that fail to close. They may even die of starvation. Dr. Steffe accuses the medical educational establishment of failing to recognize the importance of nutrition in healing (*Nutrition Health Review*, No. 32, Fall 1984).

Forbes magazine, April 9, 1984, reports: "If there is one definable problem of malnutrition in America, it is in the intensive care units, wards and private rooms of America's hospitals."

Pieter Halter, executive editor of *Biomedical Business International* is quoted as saying: "Malnutrition is said to cause 50,000 preventable deaths per year in the U.S. alone while affecting another half million patients' recoveries." According to Dr. S. J. Dudrick, clinical professor of surgery, over 30 percent of U.S. hospital patients are malnourished. Of this third, one-third have lost so much body weight that their chances of surviving surgery are greatly reduced. Any patient who has lost 30 percent of his body weight has only a 5 percent chance of surviving. Prof. C. E. Butterworth and S. L. Blackburn in *Nutrition Today*, March/April 1975, state their belief that malnutrition has been identified by physicians with the extremely rare, classical vitamin deficiency states; nutrition is therefore ignored.

These doctors should not be surprised. As long as nutrition is taught by professors of biochemistry who are ignorant of clinical nutrition, medical students will continue to be bored by the recitation of the rare classical nutritional diseases. Butterworth (*Journal of the American Medical Association*, vol. 230, page 879, 1974) laments the widespread malnutrition in hospitals in an editorial.

There has been no improvement since then. Prof. A. E. Bender (*British Medical Journal*, vol. 288, pages 92–93, 1984) is equally disturbed. He laments the fact that modern hospitals, if they improve the diet, concentrate on palatability and variety of the menu rather than on nutritional content. B. Isaksson, in his chapter "How to Avoid Malnutrition During Hospitalization" in *Nutrition in Health and Disease and in International Development: Symposia from the XII International Congress of Nutrition* by A. E. Harper and G. K. Davis (New York, Alan R. Liss, 1981), states: "Rarely do physicians take responsibility for that part of the patient care . . . this is one of the reasons why malnutrition may develop during hospitalization." Bender lists illness, drug treatment, poor appetite, monotonous menus and unattractive food as factors for the fact that 50 percent of all patients in U.S. hospitals suffer malnutrition. He does not list the extensive use of junk food. He recommends that more attention be given to nutrition in medical education and that the nutrient content of institutional diets be improved. "We have become accustomed to describing table sugar as empty calories but if we include fats and alcohol then we are on average relying on one-third of our food to supply all our nutrients, *i.e.*, sugar, alcohol and fats provide two-thirds of our calories."

Dr. M. G. Phillips published a study, "The Nutrition Knowledge of Medical Students" (U.S. Dept. of Health, Education and Welfare, *Journal of Medical Education*, pages 86–90, Jan. 1971). She reviewed the literature, noting a number of physicians who maintained that doctors should study nutrition. The consensus was that doctors should know nutrition and that medical schools do not teach it. Surveys in 1953, 1958 and 1960 showed no improvement. Nutrition was with other subject matter such as biochemistry, medicine, pediatrics and physiology. "With this arrangement nutrition did not appear to have much impact. . . . The findings indicated that inadequate recognition, support and attention is given to the subject of nutrition," and "Teaching of nutrition appeared to be scattered throughout most of the departments with little coordination."

Phillips tested the nutritional knowledge of 254 second-year medical students in New England from four medical schools, none of which gave formal courses in nutrition. Out of a possible score of 100 the average score was between 40 and 50—failing.

M. L. Ng and J. A. Hargreaves (*Canadian Medical Association Journal*, vol. 130, pages 851–853, 1984) surveyed ten Canadian dental schools and sixteen medical schools. Seven of the dental schools and seven of the medical schools had a separate course of nutrition. Dental schools provided 22 hours and medical schools 26 hours. There appears to have been some improvement in nutritional education, yet very little clinical nutrition was offered in the clinical years. In the medical schools the nutrition teachers were: dietitians, 8; biochemists and physiologists, 11; physicians, 5—21 percent were physicians. Ng and Hargreaves recommend that formal courses on both basic and clinical nutrition should be provided throughout the curricula and in continuing education programs (postgraduate). They also recommended that "experienced personnel trained in clinical nutrition should be employed to provide instruction in clinical nutrition."

Robert Teitelman (*Forbes*, 1984) wrote: "Nutrition is a foreign subject to most physicians—the province of a dietitian or that rarest of birds, a physician specializing in nutrition. Of over 700 physicians graduating from Mount Sinai Hospital in the 1970s Rudin was the lone M.D. listed as having a subspecialty in nutrition," and "the most direct incentive to change might well be the most draconian; the malpractice suit. Certainly, that's a crude method of persuading doctors to think about malnutrition. But then starvation is a cruel way to die."

One might argue that patients entering hospital are already suffering from malnutrition. A recent survey in an eastern Canadian hospital found that one-third of the patients on admission suffered from malnutrition. But after one week in hospital it was present in two-thirds. Not only did the hospital ignore the nutritional state of patients on admission, it added to the burden of malnutrition. G. F. Pineo, A. S. Gallies and J. Hirsh (*CMAJ*, vol. 109, pages 880–883, 1973) found 27 patients who developed Vitamin K deficiency in the post-operative period or during hospitalization for medical reasons, half within seven days. Twenty-two were on antibiotics, nineteen had no food for part of their stay and the rest had a poor food consumption.

Perhaps if we had some financial incentive, hospitals would provide good food. They do not know that good nutrition would reduce hospital stays, reduce complications and save everyone a lot of money. Frito-Lay is a processing company which sells junk food. *Newsweek*, April 16, 1984, reported that this company would spend 25 million dollars to introduce a potato chip that tastes more like a potato. Their research laboratory employs 350 research personnel who are working hard to develop a chip which is thick enough to taste like a potato but thin enough to fry quickly. They have to take into account such qualities as adhesiveness, hardness, cohesiveness and chewiness. Chewiness is a product of gumminess and springiness. They must also consider such important factors as fracture pattern, mouth clearance and replicability. Nowhere is there any concern with nutritional quality. Frito-Lay hopes to sell 100 million dollars' worth of product per year. If only doctors were as concerned with the nutritional health of their patients!

If general hospitals are so bad in failing to provide good nutrition, mental hospitals are even worse. In the same way that surgeons compromise the chances of their patients surviving surgery by ignoring nutrition, so do mental hospitals compromise the chances of their patients getting well.

Tranquilizers were introduced to North America in 1955. Over the next five years American research psychiatrists were puzzled by a discrepancy in optimum requirements of schizophrenic patients in the U.S. compared to those in Europe. American patients needed much more tranquilizer to achieve the same control of symptoms. A number of factors were considered, but no one thought about the difference in nutrition between European and U.S. mental hospitals. Recently it occurred to me that this could have been the main variable.

Since 1952 I have observed that patients receiving vitamin therapy do not require as much tranquilizer for control of symptoms. This is one of the reasons orthomolecular psychiatrists do not produce tardive dyskinesia in their patients; they use much lower doses. Tranquilizers increase NAD levels in red blood cells. In fact, tranquilizers have some anti-pellagra properties. The NAD levels rise higher and remain elevated when vitamin B3 and tranquilizers are taken together. It is likely that any patient with good nutrition will require less tranquilizer.

Junk nutrition developed more intensively in the United States than in most countries. It is safe to assume that European mental hospitals served more nutritious food than did U.S. hospitals. Perhaps this is why they needed less tranquilizer. This idea could be tested by comparing the nutritional standards of mental hospitals against the amount of tranquilizer used per patient day in that hospital. I will assume there will be an inverse correlation: the better the nutrition, the lower the dose.

The Role of Nutrition

Getting back to nutrition, why are you so down on junk food?

Every individual from every species alive today has adapted over millions of years to its own native food. Species that could not adapt died out. The best examples may be the dinosaurs, which gradually disappeared after being the dominant species for 150 million years. Their food supply changed as the climate, which had been tropical, became cooler and drier.

Adaptation is a complex interplay between the food supply and individuals who dwell in that area. The food may alter very quickly or slowly. At the same time animals change slowly. If the food supply alters, the animals must adapt somehow.

Environmental changes may be beyond any control by animals and force dramatic changes. Each gradually advancing ice age had a very dramatic effect on vegetation and animal life, as did the recession of the ice back to the poles. Man has had more effect in altering food supply than any other animal, but animals and even insects do alter the environment and influence their food supply: insects like ants cultivate fungi; elephants, by uprooting trees, change the flora. But these changes are minor compared to the changes man has made.

When the food supply changes too quickly animals will not have time to adapt and will not survive. The transitional phase between a good adaptation and a new adaptation is characterized by disease and ill health. This is what man has done to man. Our food supply began to alter ten thousand years ago when man began to crop and raise livestock. Since then we have gone through a series of phases, with each new phase being more dramatic and occurring over a shorter period of time than the phase preceding it. Over the past two hundred years the change in our food supply has been so dramatic it has been impossible for us to adjust or adapt. A huge proportion of all physical and mental diseases are the price we pay for this maladaptation for our bodies could not possibly have adapted in such a brief period. We still have the same physiology and biochemistry we had ten thousand years ago.

This maladaptation is so important to understand that I will describe in some detail the changes in our food supply, but first it is important to describe accurately what our food supply was like before we invented cooking and what it is like now. It is not difficult to deduce what our food was like; all we have to do is study the natural foods to which animals have adapted. The best modern zoos have done so, and, if they value the health of their animals, provide that kind of food or its equivalent. Today, with the many films on TV showing nature in action, anyone can see what animals eat. I suggest that everyone make a list of these six attributes of food and compare the food of animals in the wild with what people eat.

In my opinion, food which we had adapted to, foods which animals in the wild still eat, may be described as whole, alive, variable, nontoxic, indigenous, and without surplus.

Will you enlarge on those terms?

1. *Whole.* Examples of whole foods are whole grains, whole plants, whole fish, whole animals. Animals can afford the luxury of throwing away food only when there is a surplus. Early man before cropping and herding did not have a surplus and little food was wasted. They ate the whole animal except for inedible portions such as bones and teeth. They opened up bones and ate the marrow. The internal organs were not wasted. They did not grind grains and throw away the germ and bran. Wild animals eat whole animals; whatever can be chewed and swallowed is.

2. *Alive.* Animals usually eat other animals recently killed and still very fresh. Fish swallow live fish. Herbivores graze on growing vegetation. Lions do not carve a steak, store it for many months and then eat it. The advantages of eating alive (fresh) foods are that there is no destruction of vitamins by spoilage, no

loss of minerals by solution as in cooking, and no contamination by bacteria and fungi. When food is fresh we avoid all the problems generated by the need to store and preserve food.

3. *Variable.* Animals can be classified into omnivores, herbivores and carnivores. Omnivores eat a wide variety of foods from animal to vegetable. Man, monkeys and bears are examples. Herbivores live only on vegetation and carnivores live primarily on other animals.

Herbivores live on a small variety of vegetation: many live primarily on the grasses, koala bears live on one species of eucalyptus leaves. Carnivores live on a variety of animals found in their environment. Some live on very few species, such as anteaters, confined to ants.

Omnivores have adapted a much wider variety of foods from animal to vegetable. This was probably an adaptation to the availability of a wide variety of edibles in small amounts. Man's food supply varied with the season, from summer to winter. There was a change in both animals and plants. Hunger forced man's palate to accommodate to almost anything which was nontoxic.

Until clinical ecologists came on the scene it was impossible to see any advantage to a variable food supply, but people with many food allergies may have to follow a rotation diet. This means that one set of foods is eaten one day, a different set of foods on day two, and so on. With a four-day rotation diet the first day's food is repeated on day five. There are four-, five- and even seven-day rotation diets.

A four-day rotation allows the body four days to deal with foods it is allergic to. I consider a rotation diet an attempt to reattain the variability of our primitive diets.

4. *Nontoxic*—Of the six terms I have used to describe the attributes of good food, food to which we had adapted, this is the least controversial. Only a poisoner would argue differently. Food *must* be nontoxic. Man has by trial and error discovered which animals and plants can be eaten safely. We are not unique in this; mammals generally have an aversion to toxic foods. Probably every species of animal has the same ability to avoid foods which are harmful. This is a continuous test between plants and

animals. Plants contain chemicals which repel or kill insects. Caffeine was not developed by plants to intoxicate humans; plants containing caffeine are toxic for some insects, and so have a better chance of survival.

Animals have a life-saving reflex: If they become sick soon after eating any food they will thereafter avoid that food. This is why it is difficult to poison rats a second time with the same bait if they have become very sick but survived the first attempt. This reflex has been used for predator control. Coyotes made very sick by lamb's meat dosed with lithium will not eat lamb meat again. Lithium-fortified lamb meat placed in a field may thus train predators to avoid even live lambs. We too have that aversive reflex. If we eat a food which makes us very ill an hour later, we will not want that food again. If we eat tomatoes and an hour later develop severe itchy hives, we lose interest in tomatoes.

If food kills, other members of the species will avoid that food if it is a social or communal species to which learning is possible. Infants learn by doing what their parents do. We also use our sense of taste. Generally, sweet plant materials are not dangerous, while bitter ones are.

Poisons which make us sick soon after consumption are easily identified. These are the poisons animals have learned to identify and avoid. There is, however, a new class of poison. These are substances which have no taste or are sweet, which are not immediately toxic but do create chronic disease over a period of years. Ingesting them is remotely equivalent to using small, nontoxic doses of arsenic over a number of months or years. There is no way we can identify these poisons by observing our own reactions. It may take several generations before these poisons are identified even when we know they are added to foods. It requires a long-range view, using public health and epidemiological techniques, to identify them. Even then this evidence is not as real to an individual as would be a case of poisoning by, say, spoiled food or arsenic. It is very difficult to convince people that what they have been eating for twenty years with no bad effect may later make them sick. It is similar to the problem of persuading people that smoking will markedly increase the probability they will get lung cancer or heart disease later on.

Nevertheless, these poisons have been identified. They are the additives we add to our food which do not enhance nutritional quality. They are used to affect stability, color, taste, consistency, etc. Any processed food may contain a number of these chemicals from the several thousand which are legally available. These additives have been used for a long time and are generally regarded as safe or have been tested, usually in animals, and are considered nontoxic. Foods they have been added to have not been tested. Cookies with permitted additives have not been fed to several generations of monkeys to see if they are safe for them and their offspring. Some chemicals are considered safe because they are natural constituents of foods. Thus, foods contain lactate and it is therefore assumed that synthetic lactate is equally safe. This ignores the fact that it is impossible to synthesize pure chemicals. Any chemist knows it is very costly to make pure compounds; even pure water is worth its weight in gold.

Sucrose present in plants—in sugar beets, sugar cane, honey, or fruits—does not contain additives synthesized by man. When that sucrose is extracted from plants, purified, crystallized and dried, it contains traces of every chemical used in the process. When sucrose is 99.99 percent pure, it still contains 0.01 percent of substances which are not food, the residue of chemicals that would be too costly to remove from the sugar. Assuming that the average person in North America eats 150 pounds of sugar per year containing 0.01 percent of these additives, one can calculate we consume 18.5 milligrams of these additives per day in sugar alone. This is not an insignificant quantity. One drug, Haldol, is so effective that this quantity would keep most normal people incapable of functioning. This does not mean these sucrose-borne contaminants are as potent as Haldol, but it does suggest that one cannot ignore the potential toxicity of these impurities just because they are present in very small milligram quantities.

All additives can be divided into two major groups:

Cosmetic Additives. We have all heard about these—the colors, flavoring agents and so on added to our processed foods, such as drinks, pies, pastries and soups. A few have been removed because they were found to be toxic, but many more have been added. Several thousand of these additives are available for the food industry to use. I call them cosmetic because they do not enhance the nutritional quality of these foods and there is therefore no nutritional reason for their use. They cover up deficiencies in the food: food which has lost its flavor is given an artificial flavor using substances such as sugar or salt; food which has lost its color through processing is colored. A cosmetic covers up; this is what these additives do.

Trace Additives. These are the traces of all the chemicals used in preparing food artifacts which are incorporated into the processed foods. Starch is prepared from cereals or vegetables, but in order to obtain a white, free-flowing, granular powder, one must extract, treat, precipitate and dry it. Any chemical needed to prepare the starch remains in very small amounts in the final starch preparation. The presence of these chemicals is not known to the pie or soup manufacturer using that starch, but it appears in the final product. These are the trace additives which are not listed on labels and are not studied for their effects.

The only way one can determine the effect of trace and cosmetic additives on animals would be to feed the final processed food to animals for enough generations to test its ability to ensure good health and reproduction. The way we are doing it now is by feeding it in large quantities to millions of unsuspecting people.

Food to which we had originally adapted did not contain any manmade additives. Foods which had natural toxic substances were avoided as a result of many exposures with bad results.

5. *Indigenous.* Our ancestors had to eat what was available locally. There was no way they could import food grown far away in regions climatically very different. This only became possible when man solved the problem of transportation. Today, any market in the U.S.A. will have foods imported from almost every region on earth. The main problem is north-south, not east-west. Tropical food is probably similar whether grown in Africa or the Americas, if soils and amount of soil moisture are

similar. However, foods grown in temperate zones are different from tropical foods because they have to be cold-adapted. The cooler the region, the greater the requirement for adaptation. Plants and animals do this by lowering their freezing point to be able to resist freezing better. They do this by increasing their amount of unsaturated fatty acids compared to saturated fatty acids. The most unsaturated fatty acids are the Omega-3 EFA (essential fatty acids). One would expect that animals, plants and people in the same region would be similarly cold-adapted. If people in cold regions do not eat enough cold-adapted foods they will be deficient in Omega-3 EFA. According to Rudin, this is a major cause of substrate pellagra in industrialized peoples. This is a disease pandemic responsible for an enormous number of physical and psychiatric diseases. Northern peoples living primarily on tropical foods will not adapt as well to cold climates. Perhaps in the same way, tropical people living on food too rich in Omega-3 EFA may have difficulty adapting to a tropical climate. Indigenous food is that grown in climates comparable to the ones its consumers live in.

6. *No Surplus.* Early man did not have a surplus of food before the discovery of agriculture. Men and women had to work for their food. It may not have been hard work except for short bursts of energy, but it required steady toil to gather vegetables and animal food. It has been estimated that our ancestors were able to gather enough food each day with two hours of work. This estimate was based upon experiments by anthropologists seeking to re-create ancient times. If that is true, man had more leisure time then than do most of us today—but then our needs have become much greater.

Without an abundance of food, combined with their need to work for it, it is unlikely that there were many obese people. The !Kung, studied in their native state, were lean and healthy, but forced into villages and taken away from their hunting/gathering, they have become obese and ill.

Animal studies show that they live longer if fed diets which keep them lean.

We can use these six descriptions to classify the quality of foods in an ideal situation, but obviously we don't live in an ideal world. It is difficult to eat whole foods. We do not eat live meat or even raw meat or fish, with a few exceptions. It is impossible to ensure no additives will enter the food chain. Man will not give up importing foods from other regions and we do not like to live with no surplus; no one can recommend a famine.

We can devise a rating system, positive and negative, according to which food which has all these six attributes will rate a "perfect six." Food which has none of these attributes will be a "zero" food; as positive food attributes (F) are replaced with negative "junk" ones (J), the value approaches zero.

	AGES					
Food "F"	Before Fire	Fire	Agriculture	Processing	Chemical	Junk "J"
Whole	F	F	F	J	J	*Artifact*
Alive	F	J	J	J	J	*Dead*
Variable	F	F	J	J	J	*Monotonous*
Nontoxic	F	F	F	J	J	*Toxic*
Indigenous	F	F	F	F	J	*Exotic*
No surplus	F	F	F	F	J	*Surplus*
Food Values	6	5	4	2	0	

Can you tell me how we gradually changed our food supply from good to junk?

These changes in our food supply from a six to zero did not occur overnight. It required perhaps half a million years. It is possible to divide that long period into ages (1) before fire, (2) fire, (3) agriculture, (4) processing, (5) chemistry.

AGE BEFORE FIRE (BEFORE 500,000 B.C.)

Fire was the first invention of food processing, the first tool developed by the first chemists. Fire/heat has both advantag~s and disadvantages. Advantages include making food easier to chew (meat), more digestible (grains, bones) and probably safer by destroying bacteria, fungi and parasites. It also has disadvantages, including destruction of vitamins, solution of vitamins and minerals into cooking water, denaturation of proteins and oxidation of fats and proteins. Raw meat and fish would be much healthier, if free of pathogenic organisms.

AGE OF FIRE (500,000 B.C. TO NOW)

On balance, the use of heat did not damage us very much. It was seldom combined with chemicals which make the effect of heat even more devastating. Also, we had many more years during which we could adapt to the use of heat. During most of the age of fire, food could be classed as having 5 points for food and 1, *i.e.*, heat, for junk.

AGE OF AGRICULTURE (8,000 B.C. TO NOW)

Agriculture developed about 10,000 years ago. Man learned how to grow crops and how to herd cattle, sheep, goats, horses, dogs and other animals. It is likely the elements of knowledge were available long before, but were not needed until the population explosion created more demand. I would assume both population growth and agriculture developed in close association.

Agriculture distorted our food supply even more. Food lost its variability as man concentrated more and more on single crops. Monoculture developed until today only a few cereal corps feed earth's entire population.

During each age, changes began gradually at the beginning and increased in tempo as the age progressed. Changes in agricultural practices have accelerated very quickly over the past two centuries. The food in this period, before the onset of the following one, would be rated 4, with two junk categories, *i.e.*, for not being alive or variable.

AGE OF FOOD PROCESSING (FROM 1 A.D. TO TODAY)

Even 2000 years ago there was very little processing. Grains were ground with crude tools and sifted with crude sieves. It was very difficult to create the type of white flour we have today. Being hard to make, it was also expensive and was reserved for those few who could afford it. Starch was also processed into alcohol. Cooking was probably pretty well developed. Poisonous additives such as lead came into use, but people were not aware then that they were toxic. They were probably no more ignorant than we are about the additives our food industry uses. It is doubtful that processing was well advanced, and what was done was not as injurious as it is today. People were more dependent on their own food preparation.

Processing reduced food to status 2. It was no longer whole, alive, variable and nontoxic.

Over the 2000 years processing took over very slowly until about 1800 when modern roller mills were created for grinding wheat and other grains. After 1800 there was also a major increase in the incidence of the diseases of civilization. Sugar consumption began to increase rapidly.

THE CHEMICAL AGE (1800 A.D. TO NOW)

Chemistry really got going after 1800 and has developed very quickly in the past fifty years. The food industry can now develop any type of food it feels will sell entirely from food artifacts. In 1945 perhaps 25 percent of our food was processed and chemicalized. Today it is closer to 75 percent. Many people live almost entirely on processed food. Even our institutions, whose main concern is healing the sick, are happily moving as rapidly as possible into this modern era of providing junk food. In the U.S.A. alone perhaps 500,000 patients in hospital are malnourished and their treatment is compromised.

Modern processed food will score 0, for none of the six attributes of the food we had adapted to can be applied. To put it another way, it scores the maximum, 6, for junk.

How would you describe our modern high-tech diet?

For each attribute of good food, I have used words which mean the opposite. The six attributes of junk food are artifact, dead, monotonous, toxic, exotic and too much.

ARTIFACT

An artifact is a product which appears to be food but does not have the qualities of the food it appears to be. It is made up in whole or part from other artifacts. Wheat is ground and separated into flour, bran and germ. Flour is deficient in those nutrients left in the bran and germ and therefore can not sustain life by itself. The flour is further fractionated into starch and protein. These are almost entirely devoid of other important nutrients.

Sucrose is extracted from sugar cane and sugar beet and is devoid of all the essential nutrients, yet it is a major component of our diet. About 160 pounds per person per year is consumed.

Artifacts can not nourish life by themselves. If they make up a very small proportion of one's diet, the rest of the food may provide enough of the essential nutrients to compensate for the deficit created by eating the artifact. As the proportion of artifact increases it becomes more and more difficult for the nonartifact portion of the diet to make up for the artifact. There is no safe limit. Some time ago, Prof. E. Cheraskin established that the optimum quantity of sugar in our diet is none at all. This must surely apply to all the artifacts.

During the war years 1914 to 1918 and 1939 to 1945, the consumption of sugar and white flour decreased markedly in Great Britain. During those years there was an equally dramatic decrease in the incidence of physical and psychiatric disease.

Any food mixture containing artifact becomes artifact. Wholewheat bread diluted with white flour becomes artifact. As the proportion of white flour goes up, so does the artifact nature of the bread.

DEAD

The opposite of life is death. When any living tissue dies, it promptly begins to deteriorate due to enzymatic degradation, bacterial action and oxidation. Fish kept at room temperature for a few hours loses its thiamine; an enzyme, thiaminase, rapidly destroys this vitamin. This fish, if fed to seals, will cause a thiamine deficiency. If living tissue did not deteriorate it would not matter if it were dead for a long time. Eating food which is alive or which has been recently alive, as animals do, avoids all the problems associated with storage and deterioration.

There are many ways of decreasing the destruction of food value due to storage. The best way is to keep the food cold, as this slows the rate of deterioration, though not preventing it. Another way is to preserve the food by heat and storage in airtight containers, cans or bottles. Another way is to heat treat the food to destroy enzymes which destroy food and to kill bacteria which could ferment it. Finally, one can add chemicals which discourage growth of yeast, fungi or bacteria. This includes making preserves and jams. Some artifacts are treated by a number of processes. French fries are extracted with warm water to remove water-soluble enzymes, then with solvent. Then they are frozen, stored, and eventually boiled in oil. A nutritious food, the potato, is converted into potato starch soaked in oil.

The deader the food, the longer it will keep. I often think the food industry is aiming at a food that will keep forever.

Dead food is junk because it is deteriorated. The deader it is, the junkier it is.

Ideally, we should eat only live food as do other mammals in their natural state, but as this is impossible we should at least start our meal preparation with live food or food which has been alive recently. The food we bring into our kitchen should include fresh vegetables and fruit, whole grain cereals, fresh fish, and fresh meat. If it is impossible to obtain these, the next best are frozen meat and fish products.

When we cook our food, we should use lower temperatures and less cooking time, as far as is consistent with sanitation. Food should be cooked enough to destroy parasites and bacteria. Boiling in water is better than pressure cooking, which is better than roasting. The worst way of cooking food is by frying. Frying food burns the outer portion and forms carcinogenic substances from the amino acids and sugars present in the food.

MONOTONOUS

Modern food is monotonous. This will surprise people who walk through a supermarket surrounded by over ten thousand items of food. However, it is mostly show. The hundred different breakfast foods do not represent one hundred different foods. All are made from wheat, corn or oats, supplemented by sugar and additives. Our diet is composed largely of a few staple foods such as wheat, sugar, meat, dairy products, potatoes, onions and corn. There is still a large variety of vegetables and fruit. Most people would do well to shop only around the outer walls of any supermarket where one finds the refrigerated fresh foods. Extreme examples of monotonous diets would be the potato diet of Ireland, the corn diets which caused the great pellagra pandemics, and the sugar/white flour diets of modern society.

These monotonous diets are probably responsible for the prevalence of allergies. Usually patients, if they become allergic, become allergic to foods they consume as staples: in England, tea allergy is common; in North America, coffee allergies are common. A variable diet decreases the probability of developing food allergies.

TOXIC

Modern foods are toxic. They will not kill immediately but do produce chronic illness after several decades. People who adopt our "white diet" (white flour and sugar), a low-fiber, high-sugar diet, break down after about twenty years. Eating food which is whole and alive or recently alive will eliminate nearly all of the additives.

Toxicity exists not only because of the presence of additives. Food which lacks essential nutrients is toxic even if there are no additives because deficiency diseases are just as serious as additive poisoning. A diet which is mostly corn is toxic because it results in pellagra which kills even more quickly than modern additives do.

JUNK FOOD

The state of food in terms of its junkiness is measured by these six descriptive adjectives. A six-item junk meal is much more toxic than a no-junk meal. The junkiness is the exact opposite of the food to which we had adapted.

Most people need a few simple rules to guide their food selection. This was recognized many years ago when the four food groups were used to teach people what to eat. The rules were to select from all four groups to balance the diet, and when food was still mostly food, not junk, this was a pretty good rule. Now, when food is mostly junk, this rule is less valuable except to apologists for our poor diet who hide behind it. The sugar industry claims that sugar is not harmful because it is part of a balanced diet, or should be. The white flour producers claim white bread is never eaten alone, that it is part of a balanced diet. A breakfast cereal advises us that milk, combined with their cereal, provides a good diet—it is balanced. The cooking oil industry claims that oil and fat are part of a balanced diet. The doughnut is a perfect example of our modern diet. It consists of white flour and sugar boiled in oil which soaks into the dough.

I have been told by a dietitian that it is okay to eat junk food as long as it is part of a balanced diet.

The principle of balance assumes that other foods will provide the nutrients missing in junk foods. It is possible that food can compensate for a small proportion of junk, but as the amount of junk increases it becomes more and more unlikely that the food portion of the diet can do so. We do not know the maximum percentage of junk we can tolerate; ideally, there should be none. What kind of diet will compensate for the following meal?

From the milk group	milkshake
From cereals	white bun
From meat	one hamburger patty
From fruits and vegetables	french fries and apple pie

This meal is "balanced"—it has drawn items from all four food groups. Could any nutritionist really believe this meal could sustain life? How many meals of this type a week can we tolerate? How many breakfasts consisting of white flour, sugar and coffee (Continental breakfast: croissants, jam, coffee and butter) can we tolerate?

What rules do you advise your patients to follow?

It is not practical to give patients lectures using these six food attributes. Many are too sick and confused and will simply be turned off. Patients must be given simple, practical guides with just enough explanation to make it meaningful. I use the junk-free rule. The word junk has become established; most people, even children, equate it with sugar. My patients are advised not to eat any junk, that is, to avoid any foods containing added sugar. Almost all processed foods contain sugar and other additives. Avoiding sugared foods immediately removes most junk food. Later, patients learn to eat whole foods as fresh as possible with a proper variability.

I find it hard to follow rules unless I understand the reason.

Having advised the patient of the basic "no junk" rule, it is important to demonstrate why junk is bad. This is done by allowing the poison-response reflex to appear again. If a person eats milk products daily and is allergic to them, she or he will be chronically ill, suffering from the symptoms characteristic for him, say, chronic sinusitis, phlegm and repeated colds, but there will be no sharp reaction each time the milk is taken, and it is impossible to establish a logical relationship. After an elimination diet such as a four-day fast or a two-week milk-free diet, the ability to respond will reappear. I suffered from chronic sinus drip, a chronic cold for two years, without realizing it was due to a milk allergy. After a four-day water fast I was normal. On the fifth morning I drank milk and within twenty minutes my sinus drip had reappeared—it was easy to establish a relationship. The same principle can be used to show patients that junk food is not healthy.

For children I often recommend junk Saturdays. For six days they do not eat any junk, but on Saturday they binge on junk. Most children will cooperate with their parents in keeping away from junk for six days if they can binge on their own selection of junk of Saturday. I advise these children that this program is designed to let them learn why junk is no good, that it will make them sick. Once they are convinced, they no longer demand junk. I inform them that they can expect to feel physically ill with a number of symptoms including nausea, headaches, itches, rashes or any other kind of unpleasant symptom. Usually there will be a recurrence of symptoms they have had or they will become hyperactive and their behavior will deteriorate. When this happens they themselves may not be aware of the changes, they may have no insight, but their parents will be aware and will have to cope with their tantrums, or whatever. On Sunday they slowly recover and usually by Monday they have settled back down to their previous no-junk state.

I use a variation of this program for bulimics. They are advised to follow a careful, junk-free diet for four or five days. On the sixth day they binge, but on the seventh day they fast. A bulimic is simply a binger who does not want to become fat. If they did not vomit or purge they would become obese. This seven-day program fulfills the following needs:

1. Patients who cannot tolerate the idea they must forever avoid junk find they can do so for a few days. They curb their desire for starchy and sugary foods, knowing they can satisfy their craving fairly soon.

2. The binge day satisfies their craving for sweets, but it also may make them ill. This is a direct demonstration of the toxic properties of the junk food. They must not vomit after this binge and this breaks the habit.

3. The fast keeps them from gaining weight and provides a form of penance for having binged, relieving anxiety and guilt.

Using this simple approach, bulimics have stopped binging and have learned to eat wisely. One patient reported she found it increasingly distasteful to binge so that one Friday the idea ran through her mind, "Oh, God, another binge day. How can I get through it?" Eventually they stop binging.

Children and adults after a while will forget how toxic the junk food was and will try to eat it again. There are two critical periods: children tend to relapse in September after the summer break when they have escaped some parental control. They also have short-lived relapses after Hallowe'en and after parties. Teachers tell me they pray Hallowe'en will fall on a Friday. Adults relapse in January following the Christmas holidays. I am usually very pleased when I am consulted again during such a relapse because I can encourage them to be aware of the junk/discomfort relationship. I believe every person should reawaken the toxic aversive reaction by making himself sick with junk. Eventually they have no further interest in junk or they will discover that sometimes they can have a small portion of junk without a relapse. They discover the limits of their tolerance, the load of junk they can tolerate safely.

What are your two main rules about eating?

1. Eat no junk.
2. Eat no foods which make you sick.

These two rules will not provide you with grade 6 food but will bring your diet much closer to the mark. It will force your diet to include more whole foods, it will be fresher since more vegetables will be needed to provide calories to replace the junk calories lost. It will be more variable and less toxic, and it will be more difficult to eat too much. It might bring the grade of food from 0 to 3 or 4. This would be a tremendous improvement. It has made thousands of my patients well and will do so for most people who follow these rules. My food rules will follow the golden rule of medicine, *primum non nocere*, "first do no harm."

Dr. Hoffer, I'm from Missouri. Can you show me how bad food ensures bad health?

The conclusions I have arrived at after 35 years of practice are an amalgamation of the studies and reports of a large number of clinicians in medicine and nutrition and of my own observations from thirty years of nutritional medical practice. I have not referenced every statement, as this is not a Ph.D. treatise. I am therefore listing at the end of this book the names and contributions of these nutritional scientists who have helped my patients by making me more intelligent about the relationship of food to health. I thank every one of my teachers, most of whom I know as colleagues and friends.

The Medical Model
and Schizophrenia

Dr. Hoffer, you've mentioned the "Medical Model" a number of times. I'll assume it isn't a plastic figure that opens up to show the organs or nervous system, but just what is it and why is it important, especially in dealing with schizophrenia?

The Medical Model is a way of organizing experience related to illness so as to arrive at appropriate methods of dealing with it. It is particularly important in schizophrenia, since unacceptable behavior is so characteristic of the disease, and there is the consequent danger that inappropriate means, such as resort to the criminal justice system, social and family pressure—or for that matter psychoanalysis—will be used.

The Medical Model began when the first person advised a second person who did not feel well what to do about it. We will never know when that happened, perhaps 50,000 years ago, perhaps earlier. Perhaps it is a characteristic of mammals, as there are documented cases of one animal looking after another. Most likely the first doctors were healers and priests or shamans or holy persons. The Medical Model survived because it was advantageous in an evolutionary sense to the community practicing it. It is one of the most common human relationships enshrined in law, yet very few people think about it. Children, especially those who are ill, soon learn their role as a patient. This was easier when sickness and death were much more prevalent, for it is the threat of death which makes patients compliant and ready to follow advice they would normally find objectionable. Children from families which have experienced no serious illnesses are not as familiar with the patient role and may have difficulty with it if, as an adult, they become sick. Medical students soon become familiar with the doctor's part of the patient/doctor relationship, but if they have not experienced serious diseases themselves may be unfamiliar with the patient's role. Many doctors do not think much about the medical role, and even less about the doctor/patient relationship. Superb clinicians have a flair for this role. Unfortunately, medical schools do not teach these vital aspects of the practice of medicine and leave it to their graduates to develop their clinical skills.

Siegler and Osmond, in their excellent, classic book, *Models of Madness, Models of Medicine* (Macmillan Publishing Co., Inc., New York, 1974), define the Medical Model as, "the use of Aesculapian Authority to confer the sick role." The Medical Model serves two main functions: it provides "a way of organizing and conserving knowledge about disease and its treatment and so enables us to save human lives," and it "reduces the social disaster which would occur if all the illnesses of an individual or a group were perceived as being due to someone's error or malice."

So it's a way of not looking for someone to blame but concentrating on what to do about whatever the problem is—that's good. What was that about Aesculapian Authority?

That's a term T. T. Patterson applied to the kind of authority doctors are given in the Medical Model, "to persuade certain people that they are sick and must submit to treatment and curtail their normal activities and that neither they nor anyone else is to be blamed for their illness." This authority can be described as having three aspects, sapiental, moral and charismatic. This means that the doctor is perceived as knowing what illness is and what to do about it, as being honorable and well-intentioned, as expressed in the Hippocratic Oath, and—a reflection of the original oneness of medicine and religion—as having just a touch of control over the unknown and unknowable factors in illness.

The doctor uses this authority to confer the sick role, which begins with diagnosis, absolves the patient and families of blame and involves the patient in the process of treatment in accordance with a set of rights and responsibilities applying to patient, doctors and other medical personnel, and society as a whole.

I hadn't realized it was such a complex business being sick, even with schizophrenia. I can see anyhow that the diagnosis part can be difficult—it took me long enough to be diagnosed as being schizophrenic, and I still don't quite know why.

Diagnosis is rarely simple, even when it may seem obvious. There's a well-established procedure of guided information-gathering, including tests if necessary, and codification of the information obtained. One thing that can complicate the process, especially in psychiatric disorders, is false information from the patient, such as the manufacture of symptoms, or malingering. Unless there is strong reason to believe this is happening, the doctor will assume the patient is truthful, which makes actual malingering very damaging.

Unfortunately, psychoanalytically oriented psychiatrists in particular have had a tendency not to accept at face value what their patients told them, believing that they were controlled by unconscious drives which made them experience and complain of symptoms which are not really there. A paranoid, say, would be looked on as really a subconscious homosexual—though there was never any evidence for this—to the obvious detriment of his treatment prospects.

Then diagnosis is really the business of getting at the cause of the disease?

No, identifying it. The cause—etioligy is the medical term—follows once that is done, but also isn't simple. For any disease there is more than one cause—even such a seemingly clear-cut one as pneumococcal pneumonia has a whole range of them, from the necessary overgrowth of pneumococci right down to possibly psychological factors. However, in treating a disease it isn't necessary to know all the causes, but the treatable ones, starting with the most treatable, which in this case is the pneumococcus bacteria, which can be got at with penicillin if they're sensitive to it. If that should work and doesn't, you look for the other causes and deal with them.

Is behavior an important consideration in the Medical Model?

Especially so in psychiatric disease in children and adults. Of the four main parameters of mental examination—perception, thought, mood and behavior—the examination of the first two depends almost entirely on the patient reporting and discussing experiences and ideas. Mood can be guessed by the patient's demeanor and behavior. Most diseases can be diagnosed without observing behavioral changes, but in children, and in adults who refuse to or cannot communicate, or who are paranoid, behavior can become the only data from which diagnosis can be made.

Observation of the patient's behavior begins as soon as the patient is first seen by the physician. Dress, demeanor, gait and general movement are all observed. The patient's response to questions verbal and nonverbal is continually observed. The interaction to other family members is important, especially for children. Observing a close relative will give a good indication of the severity of the illness; a hyperactive child is usually accompanied by an exhausted, irritable parent. I can estimate the severity of the condition, and response to treatment, by seeing the parent. As the child recovers the parent becomes relaxed and loses those lines of facial tension and fatigue.

Information about behavior is obtained from reliable relatives, friends if they come with the patient, or from anyone who has any significant contact with them. Walter Alvarez advised physicians to have spouses in the office when examining patients, especially if they are addicts or alcoholics. I agree with this wise clinician's advice, because then the patient is much more apt to be truthful about these matters. The patient's right to confidentiality must be preserved, however. I always ask the patient if their parents may come in, and respect their wishes, but a surprising number of psychiatric patients prefer to have their relatives come in with them.

Does the Medical Model help determine treatment?

Good teachers will tell their students what they are going to teach, teach the subject as well as they can and then briefly review what they have taught. Good physicians follow a similar strategy. The treatment is outlined very briefly and clearly, then it is gone over again in detail, making sure the patient understands what will be done, which chemicals will be used in what quantity, what side effects to watch for and why they are being used. Finally, before the patient leaves, the doctor reviews what has been said, giving a prescription, or if giving nutrient supplements, writing these down—legibly. Here is an illustration of this procedure.

Assume the patient has severe premenstrual syndrome with depression. It has been established that she has a need for extra pyridoxine and zinc and that her diet is too rich in sugar and lacking in whole, natural, high-fiber foods. The patient is then told she will be advised to improve her nutrition and that this will be supplemented by the correct nutrients. But because her depression is severe, she will also be given an antidepressant. Then she will be advised to give up all foods containing sugar and additives and told in detail what they are. Ample time is given to discuss how she will follow this simple rule, and the doctor may even have to help with menu planning and recipes. She will then be advised to take pyridoxine 250 mg each day, zinc sulfate 220 mg each day and ascorbic acid 1 gram three times per day. The reason for using B6 and zinc will be discussed, relating this to the symptoms of this double deficiency such as the symptoms and signs of PMS, white areas in her fingernails, stretch marks on her body, acne and other symptoms worse the week before her periods. As PMS is stressful, she will be given ascorbic acid because of its potent anti stress properties. Finally, the antidepressant and its potential side effects will be described.

Just before she leaves, she will be given a prescription for the antidepressant and a list of all the nutrients, their dosages and frequency. Patients are under stress in a doctor's office and have difficulty remembering what they have been told; the list of things on the paper will remind them. For psychiatric patients I find it very helpful to have a relative in the office when details of treatment are described, but it is necessary to ask the patient whether they would like their relative to be there.

When I was ill, my psychiatrist never advised me of my prognosis. Does this violate the Medical Model?

Many years ago, before specific treatment was available, diagnosis and prognosis were the most important medical responsibilities. Diagnosis determined whether the patient would survive or die and prognosis was an estimate when death would occur. Many competing health practitioners were on the scene and they were probably as skillful as doctors were in treatment. When there is no antibiotic for pneumonia, it does not really matter that much which nonspecific treatment is used, provided it is not dangerous. Doctors tended to use dangerous treatments such as mercury salts or salves, but they were used for diseases which were even more dangerous if left untreated. Homeopathy arose as a reaction to the use of strong medicine and had the advantage that it did not harm the patient by any direct toxic effect.

Since death was so often the quick response to a large number of diseases which are treated routinely and casually today, it was very important to know when it would occur. Often consultations were called for, not to make diagnosis more precise, or to improve treatment, but to confirm the prognosis. Physicians could make their reputations by accurate prognoses, and it was bad for their reputations to be wrong. Many patients were scornful of their doctors, especially if the patient recovered and survived his doctor. People will often say, "He told me I would be dead in three months, but he died twenty years ago."

As treatment became more precise, prognosis became more accurate, but has also become much less prominent. Today, patients expect to survive most diseases including infections, surgical conditions, etc. They know they will live, but will need to be informed how long they will be sick and how long they must convalesce. Doctors are accurate in giving short-term prognoses but are not as good at long-term prognosis, nor are they as interested. Psychiatrists had almost given up prognosing for three reasons: they had no way of telling when the depression would lift, they had no specific treatment, and they were concerned about the effect on patients of a poor prognosis. Hundreds of psychiatric histories have a prognosis at the end, simply because part of the training program for students was the prognosis. It usually was a terse "prognosis for the near future good, for the long term guarded." This meant that the patient would not die just yet, and might get over the depression or manic state or schizophrenia, but that the psychiatrist had no idea what would happen in the future.

Prognosis is tied to or is a function of treatment. The patient should be given two prognoses, what is likely to happen with no treatment and what is likely to happen with treatment. If the disease is diabetes mellitus and is not treated, the patient will not live long and will suffer horribly. If treated, the patient will live out a normal lifespan with relative comfort.

The doctor's assessment of the prognosis will be colored by the natural history of the disease and his or her experience with it. It will vary with the doctor's skill and ability in the use of different treatments. One difference between a general practitioner and a specialist is that the specialist has a few more treatment tricks and can use these with greater skill. Doctors will be optimistic in prognosing if they have seen patients with similar diseases recover, even if the natural history of the untreated disease is dismal.

Prognosis may be overly cautious or pessimistic, or overly optimistic. If one is to err, it is better to err on the side of optimism because an important part of the therapeutic program is hope, it is important to the patient and is comforting to the family.

Sir William Osler illustrated the importance of hope with a story he told about himself. A patient was dying. Three consulting physicians advised the family the patient would die that day. The family called Osler for another opinion. After his examination he advised the family that the patient would not die that day. That evening the patient died. The following morning the grateful family came to him and said, "Dr. Osler, we want to thank you for your help. You were the only doctor who gave us hope."

Today I received a card from a patient suffering from multiple sclerosis. She wrote, "Prior to my leaving for Vancouver I want you to know I shall always be grateful to you for renewing my hope."

Hope is an important ingredient in the treatment of any disease. Prognosis may, in fact, be self-fulfilling. If the doctor gives a patient a dismal prognosis the patient may give up immediately and hasten his death. A good prognosis will help the patient mobilize his defenses and will improve the odds of surviving. Many doctors pride themselves on being absolutely honest and will advise patients they will die in a week or several months. By doing so they decrease that patient's ability to mobilize his battle against the disease. On the other hand, an optimistic prognosis allows the patient to mobilize his resources, to seek alternative or additional help, to modify his lifestyle, to improve his nutrition to mobilize his immune defenses. Today, doctors are becoming more aware of the relationship between our immune defense systems and our attitudes.

Even with terminal cancer, hope is extremely important. I have seen a large number of patients who were dying and were informed by their physicians when they would die. These patients were particularly tough, resilient people who refused to accept their prognoses, switched to another doctor and sought another treatment. A surprising number of them recovered.

One of my patients, a woman with severe metastasizing breast cancer, had refused to accept radiation, chemotherapy or surgery and instead consulted a naturopathic physician who started her on a special diet with supplements. She continued to deteriorate and lose weight. Eventually the cancer clinic declared her untreatable and refused to see her any more. Just before she left the oncologist's office she asked him whether she might come back in a week. He replied, "What's the point in giving you an appointment? You will be dead in a week." She then asked her family physician to refer her to me. When I first saw her she appeared very close to death, but with a combination of nutritional therapy with supplements, and later chemotherapy, she is alive and getting better three years later. The pessimistic prognosis was justified in view of that oncologist's lack of experience with other forms of treatment, and had she been less determined she would have been dead very soon. An optimistic prognosis based upon experience helped her gain several years of improving health, and she may yet become well. Prognosis must always be related to treatment. This means that physicians who are rigid adherents to orthodox treatment will be pessimistic in their prognoses and will hasten the deterioration and death of their patients with chronic diseases.

If the disease is untreatable, one should not offer hope that the patient will be cured. However, treatment will ameliorate the symptoms and minimize the discomfort generated by the disease. But there is no point in denying the patients any hope.

One must be particularly careful in treating chronic depressions. A depressed patient becomes a suicide risk only when hope is gone. Hope is maintained by advising the patient that he will get better, but that it may require a long time. One convinces the patient that there is a chance by abandoning treatment which is not working and by trying different approaches. A doctor willing to use different treatments gives the patient a powerful signal he has not been abandoned.

Where do hospitals fit into the Medical Model?

Ideally, as a setting dedicated to its practice—a place where care and treatment not available in the home can be provided. In actuality, as we discussed a little earlier, this is often not the case. Some hospitals provide a low standard of care and nutrition and perpetuate the diseases they are established to treat. As I mentioned, one of the worst failures is the abdication of responsibility for the care of the mentally ill, which has resulted in the discharge of thousands of chronic schizophrenic patients into thousands of smaller, and usually inferior, mental hospitals or mini-hospitals—a term which I'll stretch to include nursing homes, group homes, and streets or occasionally the patient's own home. These mini-hospitals tried to perform the function of mental hospitals but generally have not been given the support staff required: doctors, nurses and the other workers available even in inferior-quality mental hospitals.

It is important to list the things good hospitals must provide for their patients and contrast this with what these mini-hospitals provide:

Hospital Function	Mental Hospital	Mini-Hospital
1. Shelter	Yes	Maybe
2. Food (quality)	Fair	Poor
3. Clothing	Fair	Nondescript

Hospital Function	Mental Hospital	Mini-Hospital
4. Medication	Yes	Erratic
5. Psychiatric care	Fair	None
6. Nursing care	Good	None
7. Rehabilitation	Erratic	None
8. Protection of patient	Yes	No
9. Protection of community	Yes	No

Who are members of the therapeutic team in the Medical Model?

In the Medical Model doctors treat patients, nurses nurse them, physiotherapists provide physiotherapy and social workers play an important role, but only doctors diagnose and treat. Psychiatrists have been confused over their role. In some university centers doctors were only one of the treatment team which included psychologists and social workers. The "Chairman" of the treatment team might be any one of these professionals with only one difference—only the doctors are legally authorized to sign prescriptions. In these teams a social worker could decide which drug to use and have the medical member of the team sign the prescription. They were not using the Medical Model. In many cases the patients do not know their "doctor" is not a doctor. This is dishonest and may be very harmful to the patient.

Patients do not relate to too many doctors at the same time. They will work within the Medical Model with their general practitioner and specialist, but usually will select one as their main doctor. When there are too many doctors the patient becomes confused. This is a problem in teaching hospitals where a patient is giving history to medical students, residents, interns and occasionally professors. Many are discharged not knowing who was their doctor. This is one reason why patients often refuse to go to teaching hospitals.

What are my rights as a patient?

Every person has a right to the sick role. There is no right to be sick, since this is often beyond the control of any person. Even when the illness arises from habits or lifestyles such as smoking, drinking, eating too much or when it arises from an accident which could have been prevented such as by wearing seatbelts, or from a dangerous profession such as being a prostitute, that person when ill or injured is entitled to the sick role. Whether the illness arises from ignorance, willful neglect or from factors entirely beyond our control, we are entitled to the sick role. But it is the doctor who decides whether we are sick or not. Of course, doctors may err. Too often patients seen in emergency rooms with a history of head injury are sent home, only to discover a fracture several days later. This is the stuff of damage and malpractice suits, for if patients are entitled to the sick role they are also entitled not to be deprived of it by errors in diagnosis, and courts enforce this right.

Individuals who are not ill but may wish to benefit from the sick role for personal or economic reasons are not given the sick role. These are not people who have symptoms and genuinely believe these arise from illness. The sick role does not include those who claim they have symptoms, the malingerers, who want to use the sick role to obtain benefits to which they are not entitled such as being a patient in hospital, sick leave, medical insurance or workers' compensation. Doctors who consistently have to deal with these claims tend to become paranoid and may believe many patients who really are ill are malingering. But when a patient is found to be malingering, it is very difficult for that person to be accepted as a patient thereafter since they too can become ill and then entitled to the sick role; they may be seriously neglected. It is an example of crying wolf too often.

A patient is excused from his/her usual duties and responsibilities for the duration of the sick role. That person does not go to work, stays home from school, avoids public meetings, and so on, until there is no longer any need.

But rights must be balanced by responsibilities. Patients have a duty to try to get well, to seek help and to cooperate with treatment. They must not expect to be passive members of the treatment process.

Do families have any rights?

The psychoanalytic models adopted by so many psychiatrists led to two evils: the subconscious became much more important than what the patient said or did—psychiatrists devoted hundred of hours to trying to uncover the real meaning of ordinary human interaction. The second evil arose from the pernicious doctrine that parents, usually mothers, made their children ill, or that schizophrenia descended like a pall on a family and was gathered into the most vulnerable or weakest person. As a result, treatment excluded families and created hostility in patients against the family. Schizophrenic patients are often very paranoid, and this is often reinforced by psychiatrists who use parents as scapegoats in psychotherapy.

Families must be considered allies of the medical treatment team in healing a sick member. To be effective allies they must be informed about the illness: its diagnosis, causes, treatment and prognosis. They should not be given information which would violate a patient's privacy. Thus, if a young woman once had an abortion not known to her family, it would be malpractice to tell them. Generally I do not divulge details of patients' hallucinations and delusions. I will discuss them if patients have already let their family know about these details.

The family has the right to visit their relative in hospital. Too often doctors forbid relatives from visiting, as patients may be more disturbed afterwards. This rule should be used very sparingly and only to exclude psychotic or psychopathic relatives. Patients also have the right *not* to be visited by their relatives, but it is their decision.

Families have the right to expect that their relatives will be given the best possible treatment. They should enforce this right through the courts if necessary.

Families also have duties. These are the same duties as those of the patient: to be truthful, to help the patient cooperate with the doctor. Many of my treatment failures were in families unable to cooperate for economic or other reasons, or who were unwilling to do so. I can recall one patient, a chronic schizophrenic with mood swings. Whenever he cooperated—avoided junk food, alcohol and did not smoke—he did very well. However his father thought these lifestyle changes were ridiculous, and even though his mother did her best to cooperate, it was impossible to treat him, and he is now a chronic patient somewhere in eastern Canada.

I suppose society, too, has some rights?

Society has a right to be protected against irrational and unpredictable behavior. This is accepted as true by all human societies, but societies vary enormously in their ability to tolerate this sort of behavior. I have been in U.S. cities enough to be able to compare American and Canadian attitudes. In general I find Americans much more tolerant of deviant (not illegal) behavior. I have seen many chronic patients wandering in downtown New York, on the streets and in the stores, who would be promptly picked up by police in Canada and taken to a hospital emergency department without laying any charges. I think our Canadian program is more humane and kinder, both to patients and to society. Some of my best friends are patients brought to hospital by police and treated.

A superb example of U.S. tolerance is the situation in Washington, D.C., described several years ago in the Washington papers. St. Elizabeth's Hospital is a large, modern, psychiatric hospital working closely with the National Institute of Mental Health. It houses a large number of chronic, tranquilized schizophrenics who wander the streets of Washington. Some of them also wander into the National Library where they behave as they do in hospital. One patient was seen standing in front of a Xerox machine with a wastepaper basket over his head, shouting at it. Another patient would always end up alone in any room she entered because no one could stand her stench. The reporter describing this stated that the library had become the day room of St. Elizabeth's Hospital. In Canada these patients would be returned to hospital. In Washington, local psychiatrists offered courses to librarians to teach them how to cope with this behavior.

Optimum Treatment

Would you mind summarizing the main components of what is, in your opinion, the optimum treatment program?

The best treatment program will restore the greatest proportion of schizophrenics to full health. This I have defined as a state free of signs and symptoms achieved by a person who is normally productive, gets along reasonably well with family and within the community. An offshoot of the best treatment is prevention. One-day prevention will be as effective for schizophrenia as it is has been for smallpox. It will depend upon public health and public nutrition which obeys the rules described in this book.

The best treatment program uses the Medical Model. Patients know what they have and why, and cooperate fully with treatment, as do their families. Their doctors will be skilled in using all the facets of orthomolecular and standard medical treatment.

Treatment will be carried out in the home. When this is not possible, patients will be treated in hospitals which enhance the chance for recovery by providing optimum nutrition and care as well as medication. Patients will not be discharged until they are capable of living either at home or in mini-hospitals.

The treatment team will include one or more health professionals: doctors, nurses, social workers, psychologists and others as needed. Each member will play an appropriate role within his or her field of expertise.

Treatment will include nutrition, supplements, drugs and, rarely, ECT. Each treatment program will be tailored to each patient as all are unique. Drugs will be removed as soon as they are not required. This will be done slowly, under medical supervision.

The best treatment program will free research institutes from the need to examine ever more tranquilizers so they can turn their attention to developing an even more effective treatment program. We must have specific laboratory tests to determine which nutrients are needed in extra quantities. We need specific tests to find out which subgroup of schizophrenics the patient belongs to. We need tests to find out the vulnerable members of our society.

The best treatment program will liberate patients and their families from the horror and tragedy of schizophrenia. It will lift the burden of schizophrenia from the community. This burden is best seen by examining the cost. Each schizophrenic will cost society one million dollars over the next forty years, assuming a five percent inflation factor. If we assume that one percent of the population is schizophrenic (this is probably too low) and that the annual cost is $25,000 per year per patient, then the cost per mission of population is $250 million per year—for the U.S.A., more than five and a half billion dollars.

This cost includes loss of productivity, hospital, medical and drug, legal and criminal, and welfare payments.

The use of any one component of treatment alone does not constitute the best possible treatment. The standard treatment as used today *IS NOT THE BEST POSSIBLE TREATMENT.*

How Patients and Their Families Deal with Schizophrenia

Schizophrenia is devastating to its victims and to the members of their families, especially when the sick member responds only partially or not at all. The family's burden is made even worse when physicians, or more often psychiatrists, place an additional level of guilt and pessimism upon the family. Many years ago, following Freud, it became fashionable to blame the family directly or indirectly. The concept of the schizophrenogenic mother, the mother who made her child sick, did nothing for the sick child, made the parents depressed, and often destroyed their marriage. Countless mothers, especially in the United States and Canada, have suffered from this paranoid delusion so tenaciously held by psychiatrists. Modern psychiatry has become more biologically oriented and the delusion is slowly vanishing—helped on its way, perhaps, when many more women entered the field of psychiatry.

That needless burden having been lifted, we now find families struggling with a different problem: Parents of schizophrenics are expected to carry on with the treatment which is prescribed either on an out-patient basis or in a psychiatric hospital. When standard treatment is used (tranquilizers), recovery is usually partial. The illness changes its coat and one set of symptoms—the perceptual changes, thought disorder and mood fluctuations—is replaced by another—chronic, permanently impaired, marked by sedation, lack of initiative, lack of energy, poverty of ideas and relations, and side effects. Parents are now expected to convert their homes into mini-hospitals where they provide twenty-four-hour nursing care. This they will do gladly, but after years without any evidence of improvement, the whole family wears down. I judge the state of a patient's health by examining the patient and by the amount of weariness and depression I see in the parents. The only relief they get is when patients are admitted to hospital, which adds additional burdens, or when patients go to group homes—surrogate mental hospitals scattered throughout the community.

Parents who become aware of orthomolecular therapy immediately run into a new set of burdens, but these are eased by a new-found hope that something more can be done. There is nothing as powerful as hope in helping families cope, and when they see the possibility of recovery, even if it requires several years to achieve it, they once more become a hopeful, reunited, whole family. They even become believers and join schizophrenia associations and talk about the miracle. They may drive their skeptical doctors wild with their opinions. And why not? In my opinion one does not need an M.D. degree or a Ph.D. to determine whether a patient is sick or well. Healthy persons are free of symptoms and signs of illness, get along reasonably well with the family and the community, and are gainfully employed. They make a contribution to their culture and society and pay taxes. They no longer cost the community a million dollars per lifetime of illness. It is the height of folly and arrogance for doctors to deny that these patients are well simply because in their view they got well for the wrong reason. Parents with normal intelligence are as good as observers as are doctors, M.D.'s or Ph.D.'s.

I have selected a few examples from the thousands of patients I have treated. In these histories you will find an account of the struggles and accomplishments of families with schizophrenic relatives, the opposition and skepticism they had to confront and the final outcome. None of these patients recovered until the nutrient elements of treatment were added. These families seldom had the luxury of community support, seldom were comforted by their physicians who insulted them, considered them gullible or naive and patronized them. If placebo is a powerful positive therapeutic force, then these families were drowned in its opposite malignant force I once termed "obecalp"—placebo spelled backwards.

JOHN'S FAMILY AND HIS RECOVERY

John became schizophrenic over a brief period when he was twenty-one. He was admitted to Sunnybrook Hospital in 1968, very psychotic. He heard voices and was very delusional, believing that everything referred to him, that he could influence the weather and the international situation, and that atomic war was imminent. His mood was not appropriate. He was both agitated and withdrawn. In hospital he was tranquilized and discharged feeling better. Gradually the drugs were reduced and stopped; over the next year he remained withdrawn. Then he was readmitted in order to resume medication. He still remained ill, self-conscious, without drive, anxious and restless, even on thioridazine 400 mg each day.

I first saw him in July 1971. He was still paranoid, believing he was being watched. He remained self-conscious and unreal. His predominant symptoms were depression and anxiety. He was then started on a sugar-free diet and 1 gram of niacin three times a day plus the same dose of ascorbic acid.

A few weeks later he was almost free of symptoms and the drug was reduced to 200 mg per day. Three weeks later he was free of the need for the drug. He remained well until October 20, when he became jaundiced. This was variously diagnosed as infectious hepatitis or obstructive jaundice. Because several internists blamed the vitamins, especially niacin, all pills were discontinued. By December 14th he was again clearly psychotic.

January 1974 he was in a psychiatric ward. His liver was healing rapidly and he was back on medication. His psychiatrist absolutely refused to allow him to resume his vitamins, even though the patient demanded this as did his family. The doctor told them, "Vitamins? This is pure crap!" Had his decision carried the day, John would by now have been a chronic deteriorated patient, living somewhere in mid-city, now populated by similar hopelessly ill, deteriorated, now-and-then-tranquilized patients. But John's parents were made of sterner stuff. They had seen what the vitamins had done and they knew they would get John back on them, even if it meant flying him back to see me, 1600 miles away. The same psychiatrist blamed his illness on the family, telling them, "John was like a fluffy little bird in the nest, and not just his mother but the whole family was ill." And so they were: John was ill from viral hepatitis and schizophrenia and tranquilizers, while his parents were ill with anxiety, depression and frustration.

In February he was transferred to a different hospital against his parents' wishes and given a series of ECT. He was now on 400 mg of chlorpromazine per day and was showing the early signs of tardive dyskinesia. By this time, the physicians looking after his jaundice concluded it was not niacin-induced, but the psychiatrist refused to allow John to resume the niacin because "It would make the liver damage irreversible." John's parents were blocked in every attempt to start him back on vitamins.

Eventually John was discharged and his parents started him on niacin, up to 8 grams per day. A month later, because his liver function tests still indicated some problem, he was switched to niacinamide 3 grams per day. For two weeks before, he had been off all vitamins and had deteriorated.

I saw him again and because of his heavy consumption of milk, I had him do a four-day fast. By the fourth day he was free of anxiety and tension. He was still on niacinamide. In July he fasted again and by the fourth day he was normal.

John has been well ever since. He became a registered nurse, married, and has two children. During April 1979 he called to let me know he was still well and a nurse at Vancouver General Hospital. He remains well today and is still on niacinamide, ascorbic acid, pyridoxine and zinc sulphate, while avoiding sugar and other junk food.

His parents have kept me fully informed. Here are excerpts from a few of their letters.

May 10, 1976

It is quite some time since I have written to you and I would like to bring you up to date.

John is happily married (Dec. 20/75) and lives just eight miles away. They drop over quite often.

Since his "double" fast in May/74 and Beminol injections John has been well. He continued the injections (two each week) until advised by you, through a phone call to his Uncle in Saskatoon, to discontinue them. (Sept/75). He continues to take three gr. niacinamide and 3 gr. vitamin C each day. He also follows the diet.

After moving here with us in Feb/75 he worked in a Nursery from early spring until the end of June when the work came to an end then went into welding course in which he did well. However he was waiting to begin the Health Emergency Care course which was his real interest. He is doing very well in this course and will complete it by the end of June. He is now looking around for a position. With the cut in health care in Ontario there are not a great many openings at the present time.

Should John continue with his present medication? Have you any other instructions or suggestions?

Thanks as always.

April 18, 1977

Just a note to say we are looking forward to hearing your address April 30.

To bring you up to date re John, he continues in excellent health—continues the same vitamin intake.

In August he will have completed the first year of a two-year R.N. course. As there is an over-abundance of nurses at this time, the course is stiff, but he has been doing well, mostly As and Bs. At long last he has found something he is really interested in.

May 11, 1978

Here I am again to bring you up to date on John's condition. I am happy to say that since my letter to you a year ago, John has continued in good health. He will be graduating as an R.N. at the end of July.

I plan to write to the Doctors in Owen Sound and Toronto and indicate how you treated John and let them know it was not, as they supposed, the vitamins which caused the jaundice. John was in fact ill with hepatitis as originally diagnosed. He is still taking the B3 and C. However I plan to wait until John has graduated and has a position before I write to the Drs.

Briefly then, John recovered on orthomolecular treatment, having failed to recover on tranquilizers alone. This occurred against the opposition of his psychiatrists. His family had seen his first response. After that they were never deterred from their view John could remain well only on vitamins. The psychiatrists were puzzled by their attitude, calling them "Hoffer believers." They were in fact believers, not in Hoffer, but in megavitamin therapy, for they were able to see clearly what John was like on tranquilizers and on vitamins. Unlike the psychiatrists, their vision was not colored by theory and prejudice. A few dollars' worth of vitamins have saved Canada over one million dollars.

A JOURNEY INTO THE WORLD OF SCHIZOPHRENIA

One of the unhappy consequences of the double-blind method for testing treatment efficacy is that the most important component of that trial, the patient, has been forgotten. The case history, which in my opinion is the most important way of recording the patient's illness, has been downgraded by calling it anecdotal. Of course this is true; every story, her story or his story, is an anecdote. The validity of this history depends entirely on the memory and truthfulness of the patient and the skill of the clinician in eliciting and recording the information. Double blinds depend upon anecdotes to the same degree. Because these anecdotes (case histories) are ignored by double blind methodologists does not mean they are not used. They simply are not recorded. From reading some clinical trials one learns what the probability is that the two treatments were significantly different, but it is almost impossible to get any opinion about the patients and how they responded to the treatment.

Physicians learn more from case histories, either from their own patients or from those recorded in medical literature, than they do from most other sources. In this journal we have now and then run personal accounts prepared by patients. They instruct us about the illness and treatment, and inspire hope in therapists and patients alike.

Miss BC, born in 1956, whose history appears here, became my patient in June 1977. She was concerned because her illness, diagnosed schizophrenia, had not responded to treatment.

For as long as she could remember, BC had suffered episodes of depression lasting up to several months. She was continuously depressed from age 15 to 16. By the end of 1975 she was again depressed and dissociated from her body. She was admitted to a psychiatric ward and treated for one month with bioenergetic therapy. For six months after discharge she continued treatment.

In March 1977, still depressed, she began to work, became more depressed and was readmitted for three weeks. Seven days after discharge she took an overdose of thioridazine and was admitted for another three weeks. She was then started on fluphenazine intramuscularly. She disliked the side effects. She remained depressed but became lazy, but at the same time was agitated, had gained weight and had a gnawing sensation in her body.

All three areas of her mental state were abnormal. Occasionally she felt people watched her too much. She suffered visual illusions, heard herself think and had been unreal in the past. Thought disorder was troubling; she believed people were talking about her. In the past she had thought they were plotting against her. Her mind wandered, she felt as if it were in a void, and she could not decide whether her memory was good or bad. Depression with suicide ideas remained a problem and was worse before her periods.

She was placed upon a sugar-free diet supplemented with nicotinamide 3 grams per day, ascorbic acid 500 mg three times per day and pyridoxine 250 mg once per day. She still remained on the parenteral tranquilizer.

Two weeks later she was better and wished to be free of the tranquilizer, but she became very depressed and July 15th took an overdose of drugs she had with her and slept in a motel room for two days. I admitted her to hospital in July, gave her a series of five ECT and discharged her in 11 days. She was almost well for the first time in several years. Within three months she moved into her own apartment, found a job while continuing to get better. She still had a few mild depressions.

During one of these episodes she took too many pills and was admitted for three days. After that she was either well, i.e. free of all signs and symptoms, or much improved until October 28, 1979, when she was admitted for eight days because of severe anxiety and depression.

February 1981 I started her on a combination of amitriptyline and perphenazine. This made her too sleepy. She was then started on clomipramine (not available in U.S.A.).

She remained well but became depressed and confused when I tried to get her off clomipramine and she was admitted for the last time October 17, 1983 fot six days.

Since then she has remained well with an occasional mild depression. She is maintained on nicotinamide 500 mg three times a day, ascorbic acid 1000 mg three times per day, and clomipramine 25 mg at bedtime. On the program she remains well, cheerful, gainfully employed, and is now interested in developing her skills as a writer. She had the following admissions.

Treatment	Year	Days	
Standard	1975	30	
	1977	21	
		7	
		21	79 days in two years
Orthomolecular	1979	11	
		3	
		8	
	1983	6	28 days in 6 years

The personal, social and financial burden of schizophrenia is enormous. There is no need to point out that it is better to be well than sick for everyone. But states and provinces need to be reminded that the only way to save money is to get the patients well. Here we have a comparison between a happy, healthy, productive young woman who is not a burden on society and who pays income tax, compared to her previous, totally dependent, depressed and unproductive state. In two years on tranquilizers only, hospital costs alone at $400 per day came to $3160, or $1580 per year. For the next seven years her costs were $1120 or $160 per year. This is not a real picture of costs but does allow us to make a simple comparison. I estimated earlier that every schizophrenic treated by tranquilizers alone will cost the community about one million dollars over a lifetime. A few simple vitamins, used in conjunction with small amounts of drugs as needed, will save our community one million dollars over the next 33 years (counting from her first introduction to nutrient treatment).

Here is BC's account of her illness:

I tend to believe what R. D. Laing said: that the schizophrenic patient is suffering from a broken heart. I think that the patient starts to split away from reality and enter his own world because of pain and stress. The self is divorced from the body and the patient may even want to try to kill the self so that it will not suffer any more pain. By trying to escape from the immediate circumstances, the inner self becomes split and starts to lose its identity, and eventually begins to lose access to the outside world. When a painful situation occurs and the patient finds it hard to bear, he will try to alleviate that pain by not acknowledging it or escaping from it. Thus the inner self becomes fragmented and is tortured by splitting into concentrated pieces. The patient goes into a state of chaotic nonentity and eventually may become totally submerged in a whole new world containing its own visions, sounds and reason.

To others he appears unintelligible, rambling from one thought to another and one emotion to another, or as he detaches himself completely from the "real" world, he appears to be in a state of stupor.

Society condescends to the "mental" patient and sees him as some kind of freak. We do not realize that the patient may contain a sensitivity that is rare and precious. If the patient didn't possess this sensitivity perhaps he wouldn't be detached from us and be trapped in his chaotic state or be submerged in his private world.

We need to recognize that the illness schizophrenia should not be shunned by us, but accepted as a real part of life and our society. I believe that love and encouragement should be a big part of the treatment of the schizophrenic patient. They should be shown that the "real" world contains love, not only hate, and pleasure, not only pain. I believe that *no* form of treatment can guarantee recovery without the added elements of love, patience and understanding. Without it the patient has no desire, or even ability to come back to reality, and if he doesn't, perhaps we are to blame.

Personal History

In an effort to try to spare my family any pain or embarrassment regarding our past, I will only touch briefly on my childhood.

I was born in 1956, and, although my father was a chronic alcoholic, I was a relatively well-adjusted and contented child up until age six. At that time, my father left my mother, who then married another man who was a violent, abusive alcoholic. One of his sons, my step-brother, was physically and sexually abusive to me, and my other step-brother quite often gave me drugs, LSD included. My mother divorced this man when I was 15 and a year later remarried my real father, who committed suicide when I was 20. This was, quite obviously, a very unhappy and stress-producing childhood.

At the age of 19 I moved in with an older man who mentally abused me. I ran away from him and came to stay with my mother and father in October of 1974. It was then that very severe physical and mental changes started to occur.

I am now 27 years old. During the last eight years I have been hospitalized nine times, for various durations, in relation to my illness, schizophrenia.

Breakdown, July 1975

Unfortunately, I have no notes from this period of my life and must relate this experience strictly from memory. The changes that occurred to my mind, perceptions and behavior, which led up to my hospitalization were as follows.

I was in a state of deep depression. I felt that my mind was splitting away from my body until finally I felt that I had split in two, body (which was the feminine side of my nature, dealing with feelings and emotions) and mind (which was the masculine side of my personality, dealing only with thought). I could actually feel and see my body grow and shrink as I passed from one state into the other.

As "mind," I was huge. If I walked down the street in this state, I thought that I was ten feet tall and in comparison to the people and buildings around me actually perceived myself as so. As "body," I was tiny, thin and frail. I felt that I was about two feet tall in comparison to things around me.

I was also extremely paranoid and thought that the devil had entered all other people. I was convinced that he had taken over the world. I saw the devil looking at me through all other people; it was his eyes I saw when I looked at theirs. I even had hallucinations where the devil would enter my room. He was white and fluid except for his face, which was very real and hideous. He would try to enter and possess me by way of making love to me, and I would literally spend hours trying to resist him. I was convinced that was the way he had possessed the other people in the world—he had entered them through sex. This was the frightening side of the experience. The devil finally managed to make love to me and I was lost.

This is where I went: It was a strange and wonderful world at times. Everything was extremely beautiful and radiant. Colors were so rich that I wanted to weep at their beauty. I had no thought; I simply felt and experienced everything around me, very deeply. I saw people's auras. Different colours would radiate from a person and I could experience them and know them intimately without communication or thought, simply by witnessing their auras.

I saw lines travelling through the sky. I have lost the capability to describe these lines as so much time has passed since I witnessed them. I can only say that they were as real as the piece of paper in front of me. I felt that I had been given the power to see things beyond the immediate physical world and was in a constant state of awe and bliss. I saw the physical world as I had never seen it before—completely.

I could see movement and hear sounds vibrating from plants and nature. I felt that I was one with the universe. Animals responded to me and were drawn to me. I experienced deep feelings of love and oneness with everything around me. I was fluid, and movement was beautiful and rich. I did not want to leave this world and would have been quite happy to stay here, but my father, who was then alive, picked me up from one of my common fixed postures, sitting cross-legged on top of the stereo, staring off at things around the room, and took me to the hospital where my series of treatments began.

Hospitalization and Treatments

After my first "breakdown" I was hospitalized in July of 1975 for approximately six weeks. I was administered heavy doses of tranquilizers (400 mg per day of mellaril, an anti-psychotic) and anti-depressants, and was diagnosed as schizophrenic. The result of this treatment was that I was finally allowed to leave the hospital and go out into the community. I went home and stayed in my room for about a year, feeling totally void of all creative thought, incentive or drive.

In August of 1976 I took an overdose of my medication and was sent again to hospital. From there I entered the "Day Program," a group program including group therapy, art therapy and so on. I stayed for the first four days of this six-week program and then went back home to my room.

In March of 1977 I again tried to commit suicide and was admitted to hospital for a short period, once again given heavy doses of tranquilizers and sent home. I was determined to end my life. I did not want to live in the state of what I believed was a semi-"vegetable." I had always been an intelligent and creative person and the idea of life without creative thought or joy and only pain left me frightened and hopeless.

In July of that year I again tried to commit suicide and was hospitalized. I decided to ask for another psychiatrist. For more than one reason I will not give the name of the doctor who treated me then, but I shall say, though, that I have never suffered more in my life nor felt such resentment toward a person before.

He put me on a heavy dose of tranquilizers and I immediately tried to commit suicide. The outcome of my actions was that I was forced by this doctor to take injections of Moditin, an antipsychotic which is administered by way of injection into the hip. The drug slowly releases into the body over a two-week period. I was allowed to leave the hospital on the condition that I went to stay in my mother's home and returned to hospital every two weeks for the injection. I was told that if I did not show up for the injections, I would be committed to hospital and be physically forced to take the treatment. My only alternative, I was told, was to run away, and I was assured that if I did I would eventually be brought back to the hospital in a strait-jacket because I would be incapable of dealing with my illness and would go completely "crazy."

I reluctantly accepted the injections, from which I experienced incredibly painful side effects. My life for the next eight months consisted of sleeping occasionally, rocking in my mother's arm chair and shaking continuously. I talked to no one but my mother, and only when the pain was unbearable. My words to my mother, as I followed her around the house shaking and sobbing, were: "Mom, it hurts, it hurts."

My mother would finally take me to the emergency ward at the hospital, insisting that they do something for her daughter. The doctor would give me another mild tranquilizer and send me home to another few months of the same. Eventually my mother would, because of her compassion for me, drive me back to the emergency ward.

It is interesting to know that this particular doctor informed my mother that I would have to continue taking the injections for the rest of my life and that there was nothing more he or anyone else could do for me. He told her that the illness might eventually "burn itself out" but that he could not promise anything, and anyway, he was certain I would be dead by the time I was 23 years old, as I would kill myself.

My mother frantically sought other help. In November of 1977 she heard about Dr. Hoffer's continued success with schizophrenic patients and managed to arrange an appointment with him. After about 20 minutes with Dr. Hoffer, he had assessed me and assured my mother and I that he could help me. He also told us that within six months I would be feeling better. It was a marvellous approach and my mother had hope.

The tranquilizers were slowly withdrawn and I was immediately given heavy doses of vitamins B3, B6, C and zinc. I was given a series of six electro-convulsive treatments to give me relief from my depression and was then put on a mild anti-depressant, which I still take today.

Within six months I had moved into my own apartment and started to try to put together some kind of life for myself. Within a year I was back at work, quite happily, in the position of secretary/receptionist. I typed 85 words per minute and enjoyed a good rapport with the public.

My life went very well until 1979 when I stopped taking the antidepressant and went into a mild depression. I was hospitalized under Dr. Hoffer's care for a two-week period in which I was given tranquilizers until the antidepressant started to take effect. I went back home and back to work.

From 1979 to 1983 I lived quite happily, working occasionally (my typing speed came up to 95 words per minute), writing, sewing and designing, was married and studied the piano in 1982.

In January of 1983 I stopped taking the antidepressant again and did not see Dr. Hoffer until October, 1983. I had slowly slipped into a depressed state. My marriage had failed and I was constantly involved in stressful situations. An account of my breakdown is detailed below. I was hospitalized for five days, again under Dr. Hoffer's care, was given tranquilizers and was put back on the antidepressant. I was taken off the tranquilizers as soon as I went home and within two weeks I had completely recovered.

I realize now that I might always have to take an antidepressant along with the mega-vitamin therapy, but accept this. I suffer no harmful side affects and take the drug in a relatively small dose.

Breakdown, October 1983

During this time I experienced video and audio distortions which sometimes led to hallucinations. For instance, once while observing light coming in through a window, I saw it begin to turn hazy and smoky and then a strange white form slowly emerged. I thought of it as some kind of spirit.

There were periods when I was totally fixed in a state of fear, when everything looked hideous and ugly. At other times everything looked bizarre and it was as if I was viewing a funny motion picture. I was completely detached and was merely an observer. The world seemed very unreal, things went in slow or fast motion and people's actions appeared quite jerky. Their faces were distorted and looked long and angular. It struck me as quite hilarious and I simply wanted to sit, look and laugh.

At times I had total memory loss. I could not remember what I had started doing, anything I had previously planned to do or where I was going. If someone asked me a question about myself, the strain to remember was so great that I felt as if my mind was drifting off into space.

I also thought, at times, that I was taking on the personalities of other people. What I said seemed to be in the exact words that another person might use, and I said them in the exact tonation of that other person.

At other times I actually thought that I *was* another person. I secretly referred to myself as "Ada," a character from a story I had just read which dealt with different personalities inside a mental institution. Ada was, I believed, schizophrenic with violent tendencies. I too at times felt violent. My anger and annoyance often reached the point of wanting to give a physical blow to anyone who came near me. At times I even wanted to hurt someone quite badly or throw and break things.

Ada also would recite poetry in her periods of detachment. I too recited poetry when I felt disturbed. I also wanted to answer a question someone might ask with a bizarre poem or statement that no one but me could understand and therein secretly belittle them and assert (what I felt was) my "intellectual superiority."

I often had paranoid thoughts. I thought people were angry with me, did not like me, and were talking about me. I often felt that everyone was watching me, and if someone laughed, I believed that they were laughing at me.

Food tasted strange—almost bitter—and I was sure that everything I ate poisoned my system. I thought I could actually feel the physical and chemical changes taking place inside my body as soon as I had eaten or drunk anything.

Sometimes my movements were very slow and almost painful. I often just wanted to sit immobile forever. At other times I wanted to keep moving faster and faster and never stop.

Although this last experience was quite often frightening, I now simply look upon it as a fascinating journey from which I have finally emerged a little more in tune with the inner workings of my mind and my illness. Life is now as it was before my visit to hospital, but is perhaps a little richer and more precious. My concept of reality has only altered in the sense that I am more conscious of the fact that beyond our material and ego oriented culture lie valid and important realms of thought which too often go unsought, unnoticed, avoided, ignored and even disrespected. I realize that there is much more to life than the material world and more important pursuits than acceptance, recognition or material gain.

FAMILY PROBLEMS GENERATED
BY SCHIZOPHRENIA

Myrna, born in 1952, was well until age fourteen when she became ill while attending a school in Europe. She gained a lot of weight and was agitated. Back in Canada, she saw a psychiatrist for a year for psychotherapy. Age sixteen she was very depressed and was treated with antidepressants and diazepam. Two years later she was admitted to Allen Memorial Hospital for six months and from there was transferred to Douglas Hospital for another six months for ECT and more tranquilizers. About this time, her mother flew to Saskatoon to consult with me. I then advised Myrna's family physician to start her on a proper vitamin regimen. The visit to see me was probably precipitated by the advice of the clinical director of Douglas Hospital that she would never recover from her chronic schizophrenia. On the contrary, she improved and was able to complete two years university. She then relapsed, having gone off her program, and was readmitted for a second time to Douglas Hospital for six months, receiving twelve ECT. Following this she maintained on small doses of a tranquilizer, and vitamins.

In 1975, while living in British Columbia, she again became ill and eventually, in 1977, came under my care. She continued to fluctuate, doing well when she followed her program and relapsing when she went off. Early in 1983 her first child was born. This child was taken from her because she was unable to care for her and the baby was placed with her sister. At the end of 1983 Myrna married and the couple are slowly adjusting to a relationship which has had many stormy periods. Eventually she decided to take action to regain custody of her daughter from her sister, who had become too attached to her and refused to let her go. In preparing for the court hearing, she prepared an outline of her condition to convince the court she was a fit mother. I have selected the following excerpts from her account.

In these pages I will write down facts and feelings which I feel can aid my case. In writing down why I feel I am now well under Dr. Hoffer's care, I want to write first that I am very highly motivated to get well and stay well: I love my child very deeply and am preparing lovingly for the coming of my second child; I love my husband with whom I am feeling more and more secure and I live in a house which my father owns and which I know to be a home for my family for years to come. (We have agreed to care for my parents in their old age.) I have demonstrated my motivation by giving up sugar and more than one cup of tea or coffee a day as Dr. Hoffer has suggested. I do not smoke or drink or use illegal drugs. I also swim. I recently completed the 4D day program at the Eric Martin Institute here in Victoria (8 weeks) with good attendance and, they said, with a lot of appreciated participation.

I realize that the coming of the second child seems like too heavy a load to carry along with [Alice] but I do not work, our house is small and easy to care for, [Donald] often enjoys helping with the cooking and I am on a very low dose of medication which does not rob me of too much energy. There is a playschool and a recreation centre nearby for Alice, both being within 5 minutes walk of our house. I have many support people who know of my daily progress and who I will mention more of later on. I am now volunteering at the YWCA in the babysitting section in exchange for two prenatal courses.

I admit I was sick when Alice was born but I would like to point out that there was never any abuse or neglect of her and I always did the responsible thing, for example, accepting to admit her to the hospital shortly after the birth when the doctor said she was not gaining weight fast enough and she was found to have a urinary tract infection. I do not fault the authorities for pressuring me at this time as I know now I was sick then. I also do not fault my sister for apprehending Alice in 1985 as I was sick at that time also. I do feel my illness is behind me now as I will detail in this paper. I also feel that my sickness has not been without rewards as I feel it has strengthened me in many ways: I feel I have developed patience (especially over the past 3 years), perseverance, self-discipline and compassion for the suffering: this includes my husband who has, I feel, a problem with alcohol and my sister who must find it difficult to let go of my child.

One of my greatest supports is Al-Anon. I attend 2 meetings a week and it has helped me immeasurably in my relationship to my husband. I am stronger for Alice and am in the process of learning about children who grow up with this problem . . .

. . . Finally, I want to say that Donald and I love our child very deeply. We are both parents who have to deal with problems in our lives through no fault of our own: we did not choose to be a schizophrenic and an alcoholic. But that should not mean that, with effort on our parts to handle our lives better (which we are both working on now) we cannot be good parents to our natural child, Alice, and, with the help of friends and people in the community, build a good home for our children which is a desire we both wholeheartedly share.

Why I now feel I am well . . .

a) My illness in the past years, its pattern and genesis:

In 1975 . . . my delusions really started. I was in Riverview for 6 months and it is perhaps unfortunate that Mary was living close by at that time and saw alot of me when I was at my very sickest. I had been, previous to that stay, attempting to do several things which all failed all at once in '75.

During the next 10 years I was sick on and off again. I could never totally discount my "voices," as, coming from a relatively successful family, I could not believe just how sick I actually had been. I also got involved with some very caring people interested in psychic phenomena in Victoria around 1977–79 and, unfortunately, that bolstered my belief in my own "voices." I built up a complicated mythology around myself, starting in '75, with periods of wellness in between and it was only in the fall of 1985 that the whole situation reached a crisis and I became able, through the megavitamin therapy to muster the positive mental energy to throw off all the delusions finally, accepting the gravity of my illness and the realization that the megavitamin program had consistently brought me back to sanity more than once. I then accepted that I needed to take the vitamins for the rest of my life and probably medication as well. These ideas were always very difficult for me to accept before.

I was sick when I was carrying Alice but [appeared] well enough that many people didn't know I was, in the beginning, at least. I recovered my sanity a few months after the baby was born through following [the entire treatment approach].

I was well from May of '83 to August of '84 when my husband left me to learn how to deal with his drinking problem after having completed the Victoria Life Enrichment Society program. He went to AA for 3 months in '84. The reason that I got sick was that I asked Dr. Hoffer if I could go totally off of medication as I was doing so well on such a low dosage. He let me try it but I knew within myself that I should have done it more gradually, if at all. I did not tell him this as I felt over-expectant. Donald was in VLES at this time and I was hopeful of also becoming drug-free. My delusions reappeared and I accepted that reality as I still hoped secretly that maybe my illness made some sort of sense and with my belief in psychic "voices," which I did not think Dr. Hoffer would culturally accept, I did not tell him I was hearing voices again as I did not think he would understand that sort of thing. But mostly, when I was sick I felt very important and, being unhappy about my close family (Donald and Alice) this was very alluring for me. I still cared for Alice very conscientiously . . . I carried on this way until the spring of '85 when I ran out of medication while travelling to Montreal to see my parents about getting Alice back and decided to go it without any pills, "au naturel."

Mary apprehended Alice on my way home. This really precipitated a crisis for me, especially being off of all pills, and I finally admitted myself on the 8th of August '85 to the EMI.

I realize that I am in the minority, being a schizophrenic who feels cured and healthy now. I know time is not on my side yet. Dr. Hoffer's megavitamin therapy is the only therapy that has consistently helped me more than once. I have now accepted the therapy totally and have finally decided to follow Dr. Hoffer's care in all ways, cutting sugar out of my diet and keeping my consumption of tea and coffee low now . . . I was finally cured of all delusions by simply starting again on . . . vitamins, without any talk therapy . . . where months of heavy tranquilizer . . . did almost nothing for me.

In the fall of '85 my husband I reunited and my father bought a retirement home here which he let to us. However these things alone did not cure me. The only agent which actually did the job was the vitamin pills which produced, without other factors, such a visible difference to me that I realized just how valuable Dr. Hoffer's care was and *I then resolved to totally follow all his advice which I have never fully done before.*

b) The present and what I am now doing for myself.

I am now stabilized on 100 mg. of chlorpromazine a day which is a very low dose of medication, along with the megavitamin program. I experience a minimal amount of drowsiness and ill effects.

I have had many support people who help me: "Friends of Schizophrenics" and their bimonthly meetings; my Al-Anon sponsor, Bea, and the Al-Anon meetings; . . . my Saanich mental health worker who I asked to see after EMI and have been seeing continuously every 2 weeks since my discharge; my Bahai friends and the Bahai meetings; a massage therapist who is a friend; my birth doctor, Dr. [H.J.]; Dr. Hoffer, of course;

my courses at the Y and my fellow volunteers there; 2 local mothers with whom I share babysitting when Alice is around; a chiropractor I have been seeing for many years in Victoria; and Laurel House where I can do pottery for free twice a week (a CMHA house).

I completed the 4D program at EMI over the winter and I learned quite a few coping and communication skills there. Now my daily activities encompass volunteer work at the Y and general homemaker work along with preparation for the new little one. My husband I deliberated a long time on whether or not to keep this baby as I detailed in a long letter to my father and sister. I had been afraid of my father's reaction to this news because the fall before he had been very much against me having another child and so I decided to write it to him. As soon as he read the letter, he called me on the phone and was crying tears of joy because he said he could tell I was well by reading the letter and he wholeheartedly supported me from that point on and agreed that writing was the best thing I could have done . . .

In general, my spirits are good and I am hopeful of getting Alice home as soon as possible where I feel she belongs now.

   c) The future and what I feel I can realistically do for myself and for my family

I look forward to the new baby with great joy. Realistically, I know there could be some depression after the birth and Dr. Hoffer said that I might need to go to EMI for 2 or 3 weeks at the most. The baby could be with me on the ward as they do this sort of thing there and I would be very appreciative of that help at that time (no meals, cooking, etc.) Still, I hope I will not need to do this and I know this sounds a bit odd to the average person but I realize that birth is very stressful. I do not have any fear that my psychosis will reoccur but I need to be cautious, as well.

If, in the future, worst comes to worst and my mind got stuck again in a delusional way I would accept shock treatments as Dr. Hoffer says that is what is needed if all else fails. He usually makes his patients' stays in hospital very brief, a matter of 2–3 weeks. I have heard of mothers doing this and returning to their families afterwards. Unlike Mary, I do not consider a brief illness as grounds for completely taking a child away from their mother. By brief, I mean a month or so.

I know now how reality feels and I know how illness feels and even when sick I could remember how health felt. Even with all my problems, family and financial, sanity feels 100% better than the self-aggrandizing psychosis I needed to survive emotionally in a high achieving family and a competitive world.

For my family, I plan to do several things. I will continue to go to Al-Anon for the years to come without stopping, in the hope that someday my husband will desire sobriety. There are many things I would like to do for Alice. One of them is to give her piano lessons on our piano which I bought in installments over a period of years and with help from my father as well. I want to continue volunteering at the Y and taking fitness classes there in exchange for my work. Also, Alice now goes to the babysitting with me twice a week and has lots of fun playing there. Donald and I investigated a playschool very close to our house where Alice could go 2–3 mornings a week and where I could help out as a volunteering mother (once or twice a month) which would cost us less by the month. I want to enroll Alice in some kindergym activities which we have already tried out at the Cedar Hill Recreation Centre around the block from us. The new baby will take up most of my time, I know, for the first 3 months or so, but seeing as how close all these things are to our home it would be easy for Fernley to do them and also, the people at the Y said I could bring my small infant to the babysitting and I have met mothers who do this now.

After the birth and the adaptation to our new family member, I hope to resume my creative work on the piano with lessons. I am aspiring to go as far as grade 3 at the conservatory of Victoria. (I achieved "Intermediate" level in 1978.) I also plan to pursue an exercise program of swimming and/or yoga at the Y. I also hope in the distant years ahead to perhaps pursue getting my BA by slowly taking courses at UVic. I would like to get it in Fine Arts as I have been told by several people that I have artistic talent and have gone to art schools in the past. I also have written poetry and could go in the direction of creative writing.

But my first responsibility is to my children and my husband and this responsibility of love, for me, comes first.

E4D Day Program Discharge Summary, April 23/86

[Myrna] began the E4D program on a full-time basis January 6 and was discharged April 11.

Initially she seemed very serious and anxious with some pressure of speech, ideas of reference and flight of ideas noticeable in her conversation.

Her attendance was regular and she participated well in groups although tended to become argumentative and defensive at times probably because of some misinterpretation noticeable on her part.

Myrna has three main stresses in her life, her alcoholic husband, her illness, and the fact that her sister still has custody of her 3-year-old daughter, [Alice]. These stresses were complicated by a fourth on February 13 when she phoned and tearfully stated she was pregnant.

In spite of these four very difficult problems Myrna noticeably improved while attending the program. Her insight into herself and her illness became quite remarkable. By the end of the program she was contributing with sensitivity to groups and appeared to be benefiting from a lot of the information given to her.

Myrna joined Al-Anon in the E4D program and now attends meetings twice weekly. She found this group very supportive and helpful to her.

She has become very aware of some of the problems she had in communicating i.e. "I tend to be more aggressive than assertive at times," and was making efforts to change them.

She has taken two, 2-week L.O.A.'s to be with her little daughter who visited from Vancouver. Myrna is now planning to go to court for full custody of her little daughter.

She is looking forward to the arrival of a new child sometime in August and has made many plans towards this time such as taking prenatal yoga at the YMCA in return for babysitting duties. She continues to attend Al-Anon and her marriage seems much less tumultuous at this time. She has a lot of artistic ability which became very apparent in the program, and will be attending Laurel House Tuesdays and Thursdays to do pottery and has plans to pursue writing and music at home.

Myrna also seemed to have a far better acceptance of her illness and is conscientious about taking her medication.

Myrna has been told that if at some future date she needs to return to the E4D program for review or updating, she is welcome to.

This account describes the recovery of a very sick schizophrenic woman who had been declared hopelessly ill by one of Canada's most respected psychiatrists, who was also one of the most devoted critics of the use of vitamins. Her family's dedication to better treatment started her on vitamins, giving her the experience of wellness she never forgot. For many years it appeared as if the pessimistic prognosis was correct, and for this reason her first child was taken from her. Yet once she was motivated by the need to have her child back, she realized that recovery would come only with her decision never to discontinue the program. She received help from nutrition, vitamins, drugs, counselling, hospital care and psychiatric treatment. Her treatment represents psychiatric treatment which does not ignore any aspect of her illness. Her prognosis is certainly good. As long as she remains on treatment she will do well. She is no longer dependent on doctors for she knows how to keep well. But the cost has been great. Schizophrenia nearly destroyed Myrna, but she is tough and resilient and has fashioned a useful, productive life for herself, her husband and her children.

"MY MIND USED TO THINK WITHOUT ME"

TL, the remarkable young woman who is the subject and narrator of this account of a schizophrenic's illness and recovery, was invited to speak at the 15th International Conference of the Canadian Schizophrenia Association in April of 1986; this is a transcript of the speech she gave.

One point of great significance in TL's story is the role of the support group she developed and how she was able, as she puts it, "to make my being schizophrenic into a *positive* force." Support groups are becoming increasingly important and useful for schizophrenics and their families, and a list of support organizations in twenty states and four countries is given beginning on page 204.

Mr. Chairman, distinguished guests, ladies and gentlemen:

Thank you for your kind applause. Thank *you*, Dr. Hoffer, for inviting me here to speak. I feel honored, and a little astonished, that I *am* here; it seems like such a short while ago that I was a crumpled mess in your office, and my life then, seven years ago, is a far cry from my life now, thanks to your expert guidance. I will always be grateful to you.

Before beginning, let me tell you how much pleasure I derive from being billed as a "recovered schizophrenic." The CSF is the one place I *can* say this, and not feel as though I have to justify myself. For, as most of you are probably aware, in speaking with non-orthomolecular, or traditional practitioners and their proponents, it is almost blasphemy to put those two words "recovered" and "schizophrenic" together. When confronted with this phrase, traditional practitioners dispute it, preferring to use the term "in remission" to describe me. It is almost as though they are afraid I will forget my schizophrenia—it certainly makes me feel defensive to have to constantly deal with this negativity. This *has* been a great source of frustration for me, particularly in the past year, and I appreciate your allowing me to air it.

What I will cover in the next little while will include a brief chronological history of my illness, through treatment and up to the present day. I am doing this because this is what most people ask me about. I would like to try to explain the factors which, I believe, caused my illness, why the treatment worked for me, and how I was able to turn my being schizophrenic into a positive thing. The latter is what I want to concentrate on.

Here, I will exemplify what was briefly touched upon in the conference brochure—my present activities in the mental health field.

Since schizophrenia is described as a biochemical imbalance which affects thinking patterns and perception, I felt an appropriate title should capture the essence of this. Just before sleep one night, it came to me. I have entitled my talk "My Mind *Used* to Think Without Me." This is something I feel every schizophrenic can relate to. The use of the past tense in "My mind *used* to think without me" is a deliberate one. By it I wish to impart a positive feeling of hope to any schizophrenics and their family members or friends in the audience. The main reason I am here is to kindle hope, and to help people realize that there is a *reason* to hope.

It is important that I talk about the unpleasant features of my life and illness, in order that you may share my perspective as it is now, and understand why I am doing what I am. Although I am uncomfortable talking about myself, I want all of you non-schizophrenics to share my discomfort, so that you might better understand the schizophrenic that you live with, or that you treat. Because through understanding shines love and caring, and that, as you will see later, has much to do with recovery.

My history, as I have recalled it, brings out several factors which, I feel, have a strong bearing on why I became ill.

We all know genetics, diet and stress can play fairly major roles in the etiology of schizophrenia. Well, in scrutinizing my family, I do find members on at least one side, who were certainly not hospitalized, but definitely had mental problems. However, none of these were members of my immediate family. This covers the genetic aspect.

I also had a great deal of stress in my childhood environment. My father was in the forces, which meant our family was constantly moving, and frequently separated. My father is also an alcoholic, and because of this we were usually very low on money and food. At the age of nine, I suffered acute appendicitis, and only just made it to the hospital. My parents had been arguing that it was "just constipation again." Within that same year, my parents separated, and I went to live with my aunt and her two children. With this move from country to city, my diet took on a drastic change. From whole foods of limited quantity to junk foods of large quantity. This went on for two years, when I moved again. Suddenly, I went from a family of four with my aunt, to a family of eight with my mother and aunt sharing a duplex. Hardly what you would call a serene two and a half years!

I am not saying that my family is to blame. What I am trying to clarify, is that the stress involved probably played a significant role in the development of my illness.

When I was fifteen, in 1970, my mother, youngest brother and myself moved into some low-income housing on our own. My two older brothers had fled by then. It was at this time when I acutely began to feel the difference between myself and the other kids at school. I felt superior to them. *I never had to study, and felt a slight contempt for those who did. I felt crazy.* I remember spending classes engraving my eraser with my compass to produce a rubber stamp which said INSANE. It became my trademark. It was also about this time that I decided to go on the pill, and, although I had not yet menstruated, my doctor prescribed them for me. When I spoke to this same doctor about my confusion and depression, he assured me these were normal teenage feelings. I figured the fault lay within myself.

I maintained the same inadequate diet, which I believe was of paramount consequences: lots of cola drinks, pizzas, hot dogs, chips, cheezies, cakes and candies. I started drinking anything alcoholic, I began smoking tobacco and pot, doing street drugs. I stopped short of taking heroin. Part of this shift was due to peer pressure—living in a large metropolis, peer pressure is difficult to avoid. Part was also due to being sixteen and seventeen years old during the hippie era. LSD was "in." Most of it was an escape from the increasingly difficult reality of my life.

I tried school counselors. They told me I was having "normal adolescent anxieties." I moved into a boarding home. I went to doctors—another GP, then a psychiatrist. Both prescribed Valium. this really did wonders for my depression!

I tried suicide twice. Then I went out to live in the streets. I began to think that if I didn't *do* something, I would really go crazy. So, I ended up marrying one of my street friends and leaving for B.C. After two years, the marriage collapsed, and at the age of nineteen, in the year 1974, I found myself alone, and back where I had been born in Victoria.

Shortly after my arrival in Victoria, I met someone very special. I knew that when I met him, but never realized just how special he was, until it was all over, and there he was, still loving me. We were living together when things really began getting worse. I started having the hallmark auditory hallucinations, whispery, demeaning voices, mild visual hallucinations, delusions and sometime the very vivid illusions involved in schizophrenia. My thoughts didn't make sense—I had too many thoughts, violent and hateful thoughts. I went from being extroverted to extremely withdrawn. I would sit in one place for hours at a time. I was afraid to look in the mirror. I became extremely agitated by sounds, wouldn't answer the telephone, refused to see anyone. I hated eating. I became very superstitious. Anxiety attacks, where the earth fell away or I was pulled up out of my skin, became almost daily occurences. My hands and legs looked far away. I lost all feeling. Time slowed down. I would bang my head, pull my hair and try to stop the noise, the pain in my soul. I would circle around and around upon waking, trying to figure out what I should do. Should I wash my face, brush my teeth first? What should I do?

Finally, my common-law husband came home one day and said he'd heard about some old fellow in town who might help me. He was a naturopath. For about a year, I visited this marvelous little man (who is now over ninety). He taught me about diet. He told me to eat whole, raw foods and to stay away from stimulants, and why. He also piqued my interest in vitamins. When it was clear that he could help me no further, he told me about a specialist who would really know what to do. A referral from a GP was necessary, but I thought this would pose no problem. But the doctor I had been seeing for over four years refused to refer me. He told me I would do better coming to his group therapy sessions than in going to "that quack." That quack, you may have guessed, was Dr. Hoffer.

It took two more doctors before finally finding one albeit a reluctant one, to get my referral.

My first visit to Dr. Hoffer marked the turning point in my life. He gave me the Hoffer-Osmond Diagnostic (HOD) test, which confirmed that I was schizophrenic. Then he told me all about schizophrenia, explaining carefully what I could do to overcome it. He prescribed vitamins, minerals, medications and firmly spoke to me about proper nutrition.

I remember, about three months into the program, feeling very despondant. I just didn't *feel* any better. Dr. Hoffer suggested I do the HOD test again. Much to my amazement, there was a thirty-point difference in score! This, along with some encouragement and adjustments in medication and supplements, kept me going for another three months, when the bottom fell out of my world. I think because I had begun to get better, this particularly bad slip seemed to me, worse than ever before. I went into hospital. I had a series of ECT, or shock treatments.

About two months after getting out of hospital, I began to notice a climbing of mood. Over the next few months, many other signs became apparent. Separately they did not seem like much, but collectively they really pointed at recovery. My voices went away, my thinking became clearer. My face cleared up, my menses became more regular, my muscles stopped aching, my perceptions straightened out. I noticed I could remember things better and retain more and more information. Even now, and I spoke to Dr. Hoffer about this recently, my brain actually feels as though it is regenerating. I told him if this keeps up, I'll be a genius by 1990!

So let's examine the factors involved in my treatment and recovery.

First, my diet was altered to provide my body with the best possible defense against illness. Secondly, vitamin and mineral supplementation was essential to aid in stabilizing and repairing the damage of past years, and also enhanced the action of the medications. Third, the medications acted immediately on the chemical imbalance, alleviating some of the more distressing symptoms. Fourth, my lifestyle changed for the better, that is, not only my eating habits, but my sleeping habits became more regulated, and I had more energy. So I tended to be more active.

People constantly ask me, "How did you get well?" After much thought, I have managed to come up with some ideas about this. Every bit as important as the physical changes implemented, were the mental attitudes held during my treatment program.

1. *I accepted my illness.* A person cannot get better if they refuse to believe they are ill.

2. *I set a goal.* Not only did I have a strong desire to get well, but a willingness to work hard at it.

3. After seeing a doctor, *I followed the treatment program to the best of my ability.* This meant working with the doctor, not against him, which entails trusting him. I have always had a great distrust of doctors, but Dr. Hoffer gave me no reason to distrust him. The base of trust is communication. He was always honest with me, answered all of my questions—which were numerous—in a matter-of-fact, positive, and supportive way. I felt as though he was sharing his knowledge with me, not expecting the blind obedience a lot of doctors seem to assume. He treated me with dignity—as a fellow human being, not "a patient." And finally, most importantly, he made me responsible for my own health.

I want to stress this point, because far too often in our society, people are looking for the magic pill to cure all evil. I believe this is a very damaging attitude, and takes the responsibility for health away from the individual, and, more often than not, places it in the hands of the doctors or the drug companies. This puts unreal expectations on both parties, patient and doctor.

I'd like to say the answer here is not for everyone to go clamoring up to see Dr. Hoffer, but to learn how to effectively communicate to their present doctor their desires, expectations and willingness to try new things.

4. *I tried to learn as much as possible about schizophrenia.*
This has been an ongoing process now for seven years.

5. *I determined my own standard of achievement for my life*
and learned to *own my failures.* part of this was finding out that
I couldn't do it alone, that sometimes, I needed help. Another
part was realizing that I couldn't progress in leaps and bounds,
that it had to be a gradual process. An illness of this nature
simply will not go away in a few days, as a common cold
would.

Having reached my goal of becoming well, in 1980, at the
age of twenty-five, I felt a need to test out my health. Perhaps I
could go back to work? Having failed several times at holding a
job for any length of time in the past, I found myself fairly
shaky about the idea. I decided to start with part-time work.
When that went all right, it gave me the confidence I needed to
move on to bigger and better things. In May of 1981, I married
Robert, the man I mentioned earlier on as being so special.
They say you marry for better, for worse. Certainly, Robert and
I had already experienced the worst before we were married.

I would like to say that my husband is here with me tonight,
although not in the audience, and I would like to publicly
acknowledge his outstanding contribution to my recovery. He
was always there to help, as best he knew how, emotionally and
financially, and I don't think I could've made it without him.
Thank you Robert.

In April of 1983, after three years of successful part-time work
and two years of a successful marriage, I completed a normal
pregnancy with the birth of a beautiful baby boy. I maintained
my vitamin program throughout the pregnancy, having managed, with doctors' guidance, to wean off all medications in the
year prior to becoming pregnant. I have been medication-free
ever since, a total of four years, keeping on with the diet,
vitamins and lifestyle.

Soon our son was running around, and it was about this time
that Rob and I decided it would be good for me to get back to
part-time work. Not only would it help financially, but it would
help me deal with the cabin fever I was beginning to develop. I
found a job in a small office, and shortly thereafter found

myself becoming involved as a volunteer in the Friends of Schizophrenics Society, or FOS for short. I had discovered the group, after attending a lecture series on schizophrenia that was put on by the local hospital and mental health centers. They were looking to establish a chapter in Victoria, so I jumped in with both feet. This was the chance I was waiting for. Ever since I'd become well, I had been trying to figure out a way to help other schizophrenics. Surely what had worked for me would work for some of them as well? This is where I began to make my being schizophrenic into a positive force.

The development of a chapter of the Friends of Schizophrenics in Victoria gave me the vehicle to set up a support group for schizophrenics in November of 1984. What began as a monthly meeting of ten members grew to the present tally of over ninety people, all of whom are telephoned frequently for meetings. We have a free room at the Salvation Army, and more recently a clubhouse where we can hold meetings along with a variety of other activities. The support group is based on the Schizophrenics Anonymous model of the CSF.

Issues discussed range from employment, medications, housing, finances and stigma, through feelings of anger, frustration and loneliness. The meetings are informal, and members are not pressed to participate; however, each realizes that their input is valued and respected. The main focus is on creating a social atmosphere, where friendships can formulate and isolation dispel.

My involvement with the FOS grew to encompass public awareness. I sit on the Social Services Liaison Committee (which I will explain in more detail a little later). In October of 1985, I received a year's grant from the Ministry of Labour to train at the Capital Mental Health Association as a support liaison worker. My part-time and volunteer work swung over to full time employment, with overlapping duties.

Presently my duties include casefinding; that is, reaching out to those who are not being served by the mental health system, leading and referring them to the appropriate service if available, and liaisoning with professionals and their clients. For example, if I have a client who is on probation, I will not only go to the probation office with them, but to their financial assistance worker, doctor, landlord or family, if necessary. In this way, communication lines are open and the person is more likely to receive better care.

I offer one-to-one peer support and information on the illness and available services to families and friends of schizophrenics. I have done several lectures to groups such as social work students, police and boarding home personnel. It is marvelous to see the rallying of support throughout our community for this type of work. The need has grown, and the time has come to take schizophrenia out of the closet. The gaps in our mental health system have become gaping holes for the public to glare through and be horrified at. The tide of negativity is about to turn with the tremendous wave of collective energy that has been gathering. We, and our loved ones have a *right* to optimum treatment. We have a *right* to live in comfort, and most of all, we have a *right* to dignity.

For the future, I would like to see a pooling of all the accumulated knowledge, a cooperative effort in research, and ultimately, because of these efforts, an end to schizophrenia. I believe schizophrenics can act as a powerful force in ensuring this end. We must keep reminding those who are working for us that *they are working for us*, that there is no time for political quibbling and controversy. So that all of us together can one day say, *Our minds USED to think without us.*

SUGGESTED READING

NUTRITION

Bland, J.: *Medical Applications of Clinical Nutrition.* Keats Publishing, Inc., New Canaan, CT. 1983.

Cleave, T.L.: *The Saccharine Disease.* Keats Publishing, Inc., New Canaan, Conn., 1975.

Cleave, T.L., Campbell, G.D. and Painter, N.S.: *Diabetes, Coronary Thrombosis and the Saccharine Disease.* John Wright and Sons, Ltd., Bristol, UK, 1969.

Davis, D.R.: Nutrition in the United States: much room for improvement. *Journal of Applied Nutrition,* vol. 35:17–29, 1983.

Hall, R.H.: *Food for Naught. The Decline in Nutrition.* Harper & Row, New York, 1974.

Hoffer, A. and Walker, M.: *Othomolecular Nutrition.* Keats Publishing, Inc., New Canaan, Conn., 1978.

Hoffer, A. and Walker, M.: *Nutrients to Age Without Senility.* Keats Publishing, Inc., New Canaan, Conn., 1980.

Kunin, R.A.: *Meganutrition. The New Prescription for Maximum Health, Energy and Longevity.* McGraw Hill, New York, 1980.

Kunin, R.A.: *Meganutrition for Women.* McGraw Hill, New York, 1983.

Mannerberg, D. and Roth, J.: *Aerobic Nutrition.* Hawthorn Dutton, New York, 1981.

Trowell, H.C. and Burkitt, D.P.: *Western Diseases: Their Emergence and Prevention.* Harvard University Press, Cambridge, Mass., 1981.

Williams, R.J.: *Biochemical Individuality.* John Wiley & Sons, Inc., New York, 1956.

Williams, R.J.: *Nutrition Against Disease.* Pitman Publishing Corp., New York, 1971.

Williams, R.J.: *The Wonderful World Within You*. Bantam Books, Inc., New York, 1977.

ALLERGIES

Egger, J., Wilson, J., Carter, C.M., Turner, M.W. and Soothill, J.F.: Is migraine food allergy? A double blind controlled trial of oligoantigenic diet treatment. *Lancet*, vol. 2:865–868, 1983.

Gerrard, J.W.: *Understanding Allergies*. C.C. Thomas, Springfield, Ill., 1973.

Mandell, M. and Scanlon, L.W.: *Dr. Mandell's 5-Day Allergy Relief System*. Thomas Y. Crowell, New York, 1979.

Philpott, W.H.: Ecologic, orthomolecular and behavioral contributors to psychiatry. *J. Orthomolecular Psychiatry*, vol. 3:356–370, 1974.

Philpott, W.H.: Maladaptive reactions to frequently used foods and commonly met chemicals as precipitating factors in many chronic physical and chronic emotional illnesses. *A Physician's Handbook on Orthomolecular Medicine*. Edited by R. J. Williams and D. K. Kalita. Keats Publishing, Inc., New Canaan, Conn., 1979. pp. 140–150.

Philpott, W.H. and Kalita, D.K.: *Brain Allergies: The Psycho-Nutrient Connection*. Keats Publishing Inc., New Canaan, Conn., 1980, 1987.

Rippere, V. *The Allergy Problem*. Thorsons Publishing Ltd., Wellingborough, Northamptonshire, UK, 1983.

Rowe, A.H. and Rowe, A.: *Food Allergy: Its Manifestations and Control and the Elimination Diets*. C. C. Thomas, Springfield, Ill., 1972.

Sheinkin, D., Schacter, M. and Hutton, R.: *The Food Connection*. Bobbs-Merrill, New York, 1979.

VITAMIN B3

Hoffer, A.: *Niacin Therapy in Psychiatry*. Charles C Thomas, Springfield, Ill., 1962.

Hoffer, A.: Safety, side effects and relative lack of toxicity of nicotinic acid and nicotinamide. *Schizophrenia*, vol. 1: 78–87, 1969.

VITAMIN C

Free, V. and Sanders, P.: The use of ascorbic acid and mineral supplements in the detoxification of narcotic addicts. *J. Orthomolecular Psychiatry*, vol. 7:264–270, 1978.
Lewin, S.: *Vitamin C. Its Molecular Biology and Medical Potential.* Academic Press, New York, 1976.
Pauling, L.: *Vitamin C, the Common Cold and the Flu.* W. H. Freeman & Co., San Francisco, 1976.
Stone, I.: *The Healing Factor: Vitamin C Against Disease.* Grosset and Dunlap, New York, 1972.
Stone, I.: Sudden death. A look back from ascorbate's 50th anniversary. *J. Int. Acad. of Preventive Medicine*, vol. 5:84–91, 1978.

ARTHRITIS

Kaufman, W.: *Common Form of Niacinamide Deficiency Disease: Aniacinamidosis.* Yale University Press, New Haven, 1943.
Kaufman, W.: *The Common Form of Joint Dysfunction: its Incidence and Treatment.* E. L. Hildreth and Co., Brattleboro, Vt., 1949.
Mandell, M.: *Dr. Mandell's Lifetime Arthritis Relief System.* Coward-McCann, Inc., 1983.

BEHAVIORAL DISORDERS

Hippchen, L.J.: *Ecologic Biochemical Approach to Treatment of Delinquents and Criminals.* Van Nostrand Reinhold, C., New York, 1978.
Hippchen, L.J.: An exploratory study of the use of nutritional approaches in the treatment of suicide prone persons. *J. Orthomolecular Psychiatry*, vol. 10:147–155, 1981.

Hippchen, L.J. *Holistic Approaches to Offender Rehabilitation*. Charles C Thomas, Springfield, Ill. 1982.

Hoffer, A.: Behavioral nutrition. *J. Orthomolecular Psychiatry*, vol. 8:169–175, 1979.

Reed, B.: *Food, Teens and Behavior*. Natural Press, Manitowoc, WI. 1983.

Rimland, B. and Larson, G.E.: Nutritional and ecological approaches to the reduction of criminality, delinquency and violence. *J. Applied Nutrition*, vol. 33:116–137, 1981.

Rippere, V.: Nutritional approaches to behavior modification. *Progress in Behavioral Modification*, vol. 14:299–354, 1983.

Schauss, A.: Differential outcomes among probationers comparing orthomolecular approaches to conventional casework counselling. *J. Orthomolecular Psychiatry*, vol. 8:158–168, 1979.

Schauss, A.G. and Simonsen, C.E.: A critical analysis of the diets of chronic juvenile offenders. *J. Orthomolecular Psychiatry*, vol. 8:149–157, 1979.

Schauss, A.G.: *Diet, Crime and Delinquency*. Parker House, Berkeley, CA. 1980.

CANCER

Cameron, E. and Pauling, L.: Ascorbic acid and the glycosaminoglycans: An orthomolecular approach to cancer and other diseases. *Oncology*, vol. 27:181–192, 1973.

Cameron, E. and Pauling, L.: The orthomolecular treatment of cancer I. The role of ascorbic acid in host resistance. *Chemico-Biological Interactions*, vol. 9:273–283, 1974.

Cameron, E. and Campbell, A.: The orthomolecular treatment of cancer II. Clinical trial of high-dose ascorbic acid supplements in advanced human cancer. *Chemico-Biological Interactions*, vol. 9:285–315, 1974.

Cameron, E., Campbell, A. and Jack, T.: The orthomolecular treatment of cancer III. Reticulum cell sarcoma: double complete regression induced by high-dose ascorbic acid therapy. *Chemico-Biological Interactions*, vol. 11:387–393, 1975.

Cameron, E. and Pauling, L.: *Cancer and Vitamin C*. W. W. Norton & Co., New York, 1979.

CANDIDA

Crook, W.C.: *The Yeast Connection*. Professional Books, P.O. Box 3494, Jackson, TN 38301. 1983.
Truss, C.O.: *The Missing Diagnosis*. Pub. C. O. Truss, 2614 Highland Ave., Birmingham, AL 35205. 1983.

CHILDREN

Cilento, P.: *Nutrition of the Child*. Blackmores Communication Services, 26 Roseberry St., Balgowlah, N.S.W., Aust. 2093. 1980.
Cott, A.: Orthomolecular approach to the treatment of learning disabilities. *J. Orthomolecular Psychiatry*, vol. 3:95–105, 1971.
Cott, A.: Orthomolecular approach to the treatment of children with behavioral disorders and learning disabilities. *J. Applied Nutrition*, vol. 25:15–24, 1973.
Feingold, B.F.: *Why Your Child Is Hyperactive*. Random House, New York. 1974.
Green, R.G.: Subclinical pellagra—a central nervous system allergy. *J. Ortholomolecular Psychiatry*, vol. 3:312–318, 1974.
Harrell, R., Capp, R.H., Davis, D.R., Peerless, J. and Ravitz, L.R.: Can nutritional supplements help mentally retarded children? An exploratory study. *Proc. Nat. Acad. Science U.S.A.*, vol. 78:574–578, 1981.
Hoffer, A.: Vitamin B-3 dependent child. *Schizophrenia*, vol. 3:107–113, 1971.
Hoffer, A.: Treatment of hyperkinetic children with nicotinamide and pyridoxine. *Canadian Med. Association J.*, vol. 107:111–112, 1972.
Rimland, B.: The Feingold diet: an assessment of the reviews by Mattes, by Ravale and Forness and others. *J. Learning Disabilities*, vol. 16:331–333, 1983.

Rimland, B., Callaway, E. and Dreyfus, P. The effect of high doses of Vitamin B-6 on autistic children: a double blind crossover study. *Am. J. Psychiatry*, vol. 135:472–475, 1978.

Rippere, V.: Food additives and hyperactive children: a critique of Connors. *B. J. Clinical Psychology*, vol. 22:19–32, 1983.

Smith, L.H.: *Improving Your Child's Behavior Chemistry*. Prentice-Hall, Inc., Englewood Cliffs, NJ. 1976.

Turkel, H.: Medical amelioration of Down's syndrome incorporating the orthomolecular approach. *J. Ortho. Psych.*, vol. 4:102–115, 1975.

Wunderlich, R.C. and Kalita, D.K.: *Nourishing Your Child*. Keats Publishing, Inc., New Canaan, CT. 1984.

DEPRESSION

Ross, H.M.: *Fighting Depression*. Larchmont Books, New York. 1975.

SCHIZOPHRENIA

Hawkins, D.R.: Treatment of schizophrenia based on the medical model. *J. Schizophrenia*, vol. 2:3–10, 1968.

Hawkins, D. and Pauling, L. *Orthomolecular Psychiatry*, W.H. Freeman & Co., San Francisco. 1973.

Hoffer, A.: The effect of nicotinic acid on the frequency and duration of re-hospitalization of schizophrenic patients: a controlled comparison study, *Int. Journal Neuropsychiatry*, vol. 2:234–240, 1966.

Hoffer, A.: A journey into the world of schizophrenia, *J. Orthomolecular Psych.*, vol. 13: 262–268, 1984.

Hoffer, A.: Megavitamin B-3 therapy for schizophrenia. *Can. Psychiat. Assoc. J.*, vol. 16:499–504, 1971.

Hoffer, A.: Orthomolecular treatment of schizophrenia. *J. Orthomolecular Psych.*, vol. 1:46–55, 1972.

Hoffer, A.: Natural history and treatment of thirteen pairs of identical twins: schizophrenic and schizophrenic-spectrum conditions. *J. Ortho. Psych.*, vol. 5:101–122, 1976.

Hoffer, A., and Osmond, H.: Treatment of schizophrenia with nicotinic acid—a ten year follow-up. *Acta Psychiatrica Scand.*, vol. 40:171–189, 1964.

Hoffer, A. and Osmond, H.: *How to Live With Schizophrenia.* University Books, Inc., New York. 1966, 1978.

Hoffer, A., Osmond, H., Callbeck, M.J. and Kahan, I.: Treatment of schizophrenics with nicotinic acid and nicotinamide. *J. Clin. Exper. Psychopath.*, vol. 18:131–158, 1957.

Pfeiffer, C.C.: *Mental and Elemental Nutrients.* Keats Publishing, Inc., New Canaan, CT. 1975.

Tkacz, C. and Hawkins, D.R.: A preventive measure for tardive dyskinesia. *J. Ortho. Psych.*, vol. 10:119–123, 1984.

MISCELLANEOUS

Hoffer, A.: Senility and chronic malnutrition. *J. Ortho. Psych.*, vol. 3:2–19, 1974.

Kunin, R.A.: Manganese and niacin in the treatment of drug-induced dyskinesias. *J. Ortho. Psych.*, vol. 5:4–27, 1976.

Norris, J. and Sams, R.: More on the use of manganese in dyskinesias. A. *J. Psychiatry*, vol. 134:1448 only, 1977.

Pauling, L.: Orthomolecular psychiatry. *Science*, vol. 160:265–271, 1968.

Pfeiffer, C.C.: *Zinc and other Micronutrients*, Keats Publishing, Inc., New Canaan, CT. 1978.

Smith, R.F.: A five year field trial of massive nicotinic acid therapy of alcoholics in Michigan. *J. Ortho. Psychiatry*, vol. 3:327–331, 1974.

SUPPORT GROUPS FOR SCHIZOPHRENICS AND THEIR FAMILIES

The support groups listed are affiliates of the Huxley Institute for Biosocial Research, Inc., 900 North Federal Highway, Boca Raton, FL 33432. The list is accurate at the time of writing, but the groups are volunteer efforts and frequently move or disband. Current information on the support groups or related matters may be had by writing the Institute or telephoning (800) 847-3802 or (305) 393-6167.

CALIFORNIA
American Schizophrenia Association
Alameda County Chapter
2401 Le Conte Avenue
Berkeley, CA 94709
(415) 841-8361

ASA Sacramento Chapter
Elaine Jacobson
2100 J Street
Sacramento, CA 95816

CAROLINAS
Schizophrenia Association of
   the Carolinas/AMI
300 Hawthorne Lane
Charlotte, NC 28204
(704) 333-8218

CONNECTICUT
Huxley Institute of Southern Connecticut
328 Park Avenue
Bridgeport, CT 06604
(203) 372-0672

MARYLAND
Schizophrenia Association of
   Greater Washington, Inc.
Wheaton Plaza Office Bldg.
#N404
Wheaton, MD 20902
(301) 949-8282

MASSACHUSETTS
Boston Orthomolecular Society
c/o 132 Topfield Road
Boxford, MA 01921
(617) 887-5062 or 862-8280

MINNESOTA
Schizophrenia Association of Minnesota
6950 France Avenue South #215
Minneapolis, MN 55435
(612) 992-6916

MISSOURI
American Schizophrenia Association
   of St. Louis
Mary Duffield
Kimbler Building
10426 Lackland Road
Overland, MO 63114

NEW JERSEY
Mrs. A.J. Seidler
Schizophrenia Foundation of
  New Jersey
138 B West Amberly Drive
Englishtown, NJ 17726

NEW YORK
Long Island Schizophrenia Association
1691 Northern Boulevard
Manhasset, NY 11030
(516) 627-7530

Schizophrenia Foundation of
  New York State, Inc.
105 East 22nd Street, #809
New York, NY 10010
(212) 473-5100

Mrs. Betty Plante
Huxley Institute Westchester
1209 California Road
Eastchester, NY 10709
(914) 337-2252

WASHINGTON
Well Mind Association
4649 Sunnyside Avenue N
Seattle, WA 98103
(206) 633-2167

FOREIGN AFFILIATES
Canadian Schizophrenia Foundation
2229 Broad Street
Regina, Sask., Canada S4P 1Y7
(306) 757-7969
(through 1987)

Mrs. G. Hemmings
Llanfair Hall
Caernavon LL55 1TT
Wales

Philippine Schizophrenia Foundation
Purificacion Verzosar, M.D.
26 Ilang Ilang
Rosario Heights, Quezon City,
Republic of the Philippines

SOMA Support for Orthomolecular
  Medicine
GPO Box 3745
Sydney NSW 2001
Australia
Mrs. J. Sulima, President

NUTRITIONALLY ORIENTED
RESOURCE ORGANIZATIONS

American Academy of Environmental
Medicine
Box 16106
Denver, CO 80216
(303) 662-9755

Feingold Association of the United States
6808 Stoneybrooke Lane
Alexandria, VA 22306
(703) 281-7728

Human Ecology Action League (HEAL)
PO Box 1369
Evanston, IL 60204
(312) 864-0995

Institute for Child Behavior Research
4758 Edgeware Road
San Diego, CA 92216
(619) 281-7165

International Academy of Preventive
  Medicine
Suite #34, Corporate Woods
10950 Grandview
Overland Park, KA 66210
(913) 631-3855

Nutrition for Optimal Health
  Association (NOAH)
PO Box 380
Winnetka, IL 60093

Linus Pauling Institute of Science and Medicine
440 Page Mill Road
Palo Alto, CA 94306
(415) 327-4064

Orthomolecular Medical Society
6151 West Century Blvd., Suite #1114
Los Angeles, CA 90045
(213) 417-7917

Northwest Academy of Preventive Medicine
15615 Bellevue-Redmond Road
Bellevue, WA 98008
(206) 881-9660

The American Holistic Medical Association
6932 Little River Turnpike
Annandale, VA 22003
(703) 642-5880

Index